CORPORATE CLASSROOMS

A CARNEGIE FOUNDATION SPECIAL REPORT

Corporate Classrooms

THE LEARNING BUSINESS

NELL P. EURICH

WITH A FOREWORD BY

ERNEST L. BOYER

THE CARNEGIE FOUNDATION FOR THE

ADVANCEMENT OF TEACHING

5 IVY LANE, PRINCETON, NEW JERSEY 08540

Copyright © 1985

The Carnegie Foundation
for the Advancement of Teaching

This report is published as part of the effort by The Carnegie Foundation for the Advancement of Teaching to explore significant issues in education. The views expressed should not necessarily be ascribed to members of the Board of Trustees of The Carnegie Foundation.

Library of Congress Cataloging in Publication Data

Eurich, Nell.
   Corporate classrooms.
   (A Carnegie Foundation special report)
   Bibliography: p. 149
   Includes index.
   1. Employer-supported education—United States.
2. Employees, Training of—United States.   I. Title.
II. Series.
HF5549.5.T7E866   1985   374′.0136′0973 85-3845
ISBN 0-931050-25-1

Copies are available from the
PRINCETON UNIVERSITY PRESS
3175 Princeton Pike
Lawrenceville, N.J. 08648

CONTENTS

ACKNOWLEDGMENTS

MANY PEOPLE HAVE SHARED their knowledge and experience in the world of corporation training and education. They have been most generous in giving their time to answer my questions on visits, on the telephone, and in correspondence. I can count at least 40 such persons and realize the names would make an unwieldy list. Besides, to name such individuals might imply their approval for what I have reported or said. That would be reprehensible since I alone am responsible for the statements made. So let me simply express my deep appreciation to the key persons I have visited or talked with at length in educational programs at the large corporations. Individually they will know I am thanking them for their patience and often wise words.

The same must hold true generally for officers of the corporate colleges, institutes, and universities now granting their own academic degrees. For the four, however, that are described in detail I wish to express my appreciation to Dr. Charles Wolf, Jr., Dean of the Rand Graduate Institute; Ms. Diane Osen of the Wang Institute of Graduate Studies and Mr. Paul Guzzi, Executive Vice President of Wang Laboratories; Mrs. Judith T. Totman, Director of the American Institute of Banking at Boston; and to President Edward G. Jordan and Mr. David Bruhin of The American College in Bryn Mawr, Pennsylvania. Each of them and their staff members were very helpful.

In addition several individuals related to the subject in various ways gave guidance and shared materials for which I am most grateful: Robert L. Craig, formerly of the American Society of Training and Development, Dorothy Fenwick of the American Council of Education, K. Patricia Cross of Harvard's Graduate School of Education, and Ernest A. Lynton who shared manuscripts and papers on the subject.

An encouraging new source of information on corporate training programs emerged during the course of this study: six recent Ph.D. dissertations from the Universities of Alabama, Arizona, Michigan, Pittsburgh, Texas, and Boston University. Each contributes to our understanding of corporate classrooms and training purposes, and all are included in the bibliography. Here, I wish also to thank librarians collectively for their willing and diligent assistance, intelligent suggestions and rapid delivery. Too often their remarkable services are not recognized.

Above all, I thank The Carnegie Foundation for the Advancement of Teaching and especially President Ernest L. Boyer, whose intense interest and concern for the importance of seeing corporate training as part of America's total educational scene made this study possible. His endorsement of the study permitted me to have this learning experience, and I am most deeply grateful. The Foundation staff took over after the manuscript was written and saw it through publication. I hope it will contribute to general knowledge about adult education in its many aspects—a part of the Foundation's concern for the advancement of teaching.

At the very beginning, two or more years ago, Sarah White of the Academy for Educational Development, with initiative and perception, helped to collect information, course listings from corporations, and bibliography on the subject. Katherine White assisted in intermediate stages to sort it all out; and Susan Shepard, in the last stages of the work, was expert in research on the early history of industrial training efforts as well as editing the manuscript. Her knowledge of educational technologies and recent developments in the marketplace were more than helpful; they were essential.

Usually one thanks one's spouse, but this is a little different. Alvin C. Eurich generously gave me more materials and informative newspaper and magazine articles than I could possibly use. Finally, I simply had to write what I had learned and thought thus far.

NELL P. EURICH

FOREWORD

by Ernest L. Boyer

DURING THE PAST two years, the Carnegie Foundation for the Advancement of Teaching has sponsored a study of education in American industry and business. Dr. Nell P. Eurich, a trustee of the Foundation, was commissioned to prepare this special report which focuses on a vital and expanding education sector. Her study shows that corporate learning has become an absolutely essential part of the educational resources of the nation.

Until now, the scope of business-based education has been dealt with in fragmented fashion. In this report, Dr. Eurich brings the pieces together and raises policy questions about a dimension of learning in America that has been largely overlooked. Her research indicates the vastness of it all: To train and educate their employees, corporations are spending huge amounts of money. Estimates range from $40 billion upward, approaching the total annual expenditures of all of America's four-year and graduate colleges and universities. And the number of employees involved in corporate education may equal the total enrollment in those same institutions—nearly 8 million students.

Corporations define education and training programs as a regular cost of doing business. Under current tax law, there is as much as a 50 percent write-off for such business expense. The other 50 percent is generally built into the price consumers pay for a product or service. Clearly, then, corporate learning is a vital public policy issue.

Dr. Eurich traces the roots of business-based education to nineteenth century efforts to meet both the demands of productivity and the training of workers. Today, America's large corporations are extending those early efforts. Driven by both necessity and conviction, they view the investment in human resources as important as capital and physical plant investment.

Programs offered by industry and business increasingly overlap those in the nation's colleges and schools. They range from remedial English to the Ph.D., from short-term intensive training to sophisticated high-tech graduate research study. And corporate courses are developing an academic legitimacy of their own. Courses are being evaluated for college equivalency credit. Records can be sent to a National Registry at the American Council on Education where credit recommendations are recorded and transcripts are maintained for future use by employees.

Corporate courses also may be given college credit as a company negotiates directly with a higher learning institution. Corporate education thus gains academic standing entering in partnership with the traditional systems of higher learning. Clearly there is an urgent need to understand more fully how this "third leg" of the nation's total education enterprise both supports and challenges traditional education.

This report describes four dimensions of the corporate learning enterprise. They may be summarized as follows:

In-house Educational Programs: Today, a wide range of training programs, seminars, and institutes is offered in the workplace. These programs cover a variety of topics including a growing emphasis on basic skills. Business leaders lament the fact that employees lack the fundamentals. In response, corporations increasingly must teach their workers how to communicate and compute.

Other in-house courses range from computers to management techniques to sales and service. Dr. Eurich's study documents that such training not only is becoming more frequent and systematic, but increasingly includes courses that traditional colleges would call general education.

Educational and Training Facilities: In addition to instruction in the workplace, American corporations are building their own facilities for employee education. These places—the Xerox center in Virginia, the RCA campus in New Jersey, and Holiday Inn University in Mississippi—look very much like a traditional college campus. They have classrooms, dormitories, and recreational facilities. And yet, we are told, their ambience is different. Behavior is more purposeful and activity more intense. Informality prevails. First names are used, and the lines of hierarchy are blurred. This development reaffirms the fact that employee education means something far more than narrow training.

Degree-Granting Institutions: An important new development is the growing number of corporate colleges that grant their own degrees. These institutions are being recognized by the same state agencies and regional associations that accredit traditional higher education. They include the Rand Ph.D., and the Wang and Arthur D. Little Masters of Science degrees, to name a few.

At present, 18 such institutions have been identified. No special nationwide registry exists; some are listed in the official Higher Education Directory, but others are not. Although these corporate colleges are an odd assortment of types and hybrids, all of them give academic degrees, all are accredited or have formally applied for such status, and, most significantly, their numbers are increasing.

In the near future, we are told, five corporations plan to start at least nine more degree-granting programs in management, semiconductor design, systems engineering and business administration. And, by 1988, eight corporations propose to offer about 20 more college-level degree programs. Dr. Eurich suggests that at this rate it may not be too fanciful to foresee a hundred—if not hundreds—of accredited corporate degree programs in the next 50 years.

The Satellite University: The newest corporate college entry—the National Technological University—may be the space age model for the future. NTU operates from a central office in Fort Collins, Colorado. No traditional campus is needed. There are no residency requirements, and course work is registered centrally. Instruction at NTU soon will go by satellite to many corporate classrooms around the country. Courses can be recorded for use at the convenience of students. Occasional teleconferencing will be scheduled. Adult workers can earn a master's degree at

NTU with a flexible schedule that takes "the bureaucratic confusion out of advanced engineering education."

National Technological University represents a merger of corporate and university concerns. Corporations needing high level training for technical personnel have contributed time and resources to launch the institution. IBM, Westinghouse, Hewlett-Packard, Digital Equipment, NCR, RCA, and Control Data Corporation were among the first contributing companies. Distinguished universities have prepared courses for NTU, and as one corporate official exclaimed, "The universities are waiting to sign our dance card." Dr. Eurich suggests that this noncampus university may provide a fresh and imaginative vision of corporate education.

Traditional schools and colleges no longer have a monopoly on education. New corporate institutions are operating on the same academic turf, and new technologies have the power to bypass the classroom and the campus. What, then, are the implications of this third sector of American education?

First, corporate education has important implications for business and industry, itself. Too often business-based education operates in isolation. Programs of study are launched without reference to concerns beyond the organization. At the same time, corporate education is a publicly supported enterprise. Corporate officers should remember that the employees they train are also citizens. Education at the workplace must be viewed in a larger educational and social context. Close collaboration with the other sectors is essential, and more openness and public accountability are required.

Second, the corporate courses present a challenge to the nation's schools. With more than $130 billion being spent annually on public education, it is unacceptable that corporate America is compelled to engage in remedial education and teach the basic skills. The time has come for schools to develop within each student the ability to communicate effectively, to compute accurately, and to think critically. Mastery of the English language—in written and oral form—is the basic of the basics, and students should not graduate until this goal is achieved. One important lesson from corporate education is that the quality of public education in the nation must be strengthened.

Third, corporate classrooms have implications for the methods and procedures of traditional education. Dr. Eurich reports a growing use of videocassettes, microcomputers and other technological aids by industry and business. Someday soon, she suggests, through new technology, almost any subject may be studied conveniently at the workplace or at home. How can colleges and schools not only creatively use these new tools but also help improve the quality of the content of the programs?

There is also the matter of scheduling arrangements. The typical collegiate calendar is caught in the lock-step of two semesters and four years. In corporate education, however, time is determined by educational purpose, not the other way around. Courses are flexibly arranged, varying in length from a few hours to a week or two to several months. The question is whether schools and colleges can be more flexible and relate their schedules more directly to content and to the needs of students.

This study also reveals that industry-based educators are busily engaged in pedagogical research. Dr. Eurich says that, "Inquiry into the learning process, cognitive as well as affective, is a growing concern not only to improve instruction within the corporate classroom but especially to improve courses for the public." It would be ironic if significant new insights about how we learn would come, not from the academy, but from industry and business.

Finally, corporate educators frequently evaluate their faculty and courses. At some corporate colleges, for example, advisory boards of outside experts regularly review curricula and individual course outlines. Internal course evaluations by students and administrators are taken for granted. The nation's schools and colleges are being challenged by the business world to be more thoughtful about their own procedures of assessment.

Fourth, corporate education raises important questions regarding the continuing education of adults. What is suggested by this study, Dr. Eurich says, is a new vision of continuing education for national renewal to meet the training and retraining needs of workers in a period of dramatic technological change. We must find ways more effectively to meet the educational concerns of an aging population, too. This challenge cannot be met in piecemeal fashion. No single education sector can do the job alone.

To respond to the urgent need for coordinated planning, Dr. Eurich suggests the creation of a national Strategic Council for Educational Development. This new intersectoral forum would provide leadership and vision—not bureaucratic mandates. It would propose policies and programs for federal, state, and local agencies, and for the private sector, too.

The ultimate goal is to find ways effectively to use all of the nation's education resources—schools and colleges, labor unions, governmental agencies, and business and industry. Such collaboration is required to improve not only the nation's competitive position in the world, but to enrich the lives of individual citizens as well.

One final point. *Corporate education challenges higher education to clarify and reaffirm its mission.* In this report Dr. Eurich draws a distinction between the role of corporate education and that of more traditional institutions. Because the corporate classroom is ultimately concerned about productivity and performance, its goals are apt to be specific, even narrow. Such nontraditional education has an essential place in our society. And established colleges and universities may learn from its processes and procedures.

Corporate classrooms are not likely to achieve the kind of insight and understanding that can result when students and teachers meet together, not only to acquire information and develop skills, but also to weigh alternatives and reflect upon deeper meanings. The goal of collegiate education at its best is to show how skills can be given meaning, place information in a larger context, and discover the relationship of knowledge to life's dilemmas.

The danger is that, in a bid for survival, higher education will imitate its rivals, that careerism will dominate the campus as colleges pursue the marketplace goals of corporate education. If that happens, higher learning may discover that, having abandoned its own special mission, it will find itself in a contest it cannot win.

In the end, universities and corporations should build connections; but they must also protect their independence. The unique missions of the nation's universities and colleges—to act as a moral force, to discover and transmit knowledge and larger meanings, to engage with integrity in the nation's service—must be preserved and strengthened. As we seek to understand and respect the emergence of corporate education, so we need to clarify and reaffirm traditional higher learning's compelling and essential role.

ERNEST L. BOYER
President
The Carnegie Foundation
for the Advancement of Teaching

CHAPTER I

An Overview: Education and the Work Force

EDUCATION AND TRAINING within large private sector corporations of the United States has become a booming industry. Millions of adults, as employees, pass through corporate classrooms every year; an uncountable number more are given what is generally called on-the-job training. America's workers and managers have been going back to school for a long time, but in the last decade their numbers have increased, the variety of subjects they study has broadened and, most strikingly, America's business has become its own educational provider.

The educational agendas explored here reach beyond the conventional confines of classrooms and corporations. There are sophisticated and growing alternative systems of education with roots firmly planted in the American business community and branches spreading to countries around the world. The corporate classroom in the educational complex of a growing learning industry is a reality based upon a new concept of who the educated and productive citizen is in late twentieth century society.

Agendas for alternative education are emerging to meet the real needs of an interdependent global community. Corporate classrooms teach well beyond institutional walls and reach far across national boundaries. The dimensions, opportunities and challenges compel us to consider that in the high-tech information age with knowledge-intensive demand, educational agendas—be they public, private, traditional, or alternative—are an urgent public policy issue for today and tomorrow.

Starting from a view of corporate classrooms as an educational resource, this commentary indulges a backward glance at their historical development, moves forward to the courses and methods being used in today's classrooms, and then describes specific corporate colleges that grant their own academic degrees. The scenario is set in the larger drama of the learning industry that is introducing new materials and ways to study. So the stage setting is now in an age of escalating technology and information. The *deus ex machina* is the microcomputer with its entourage of video, telephone, modem, graphics, simulated voice, and satellites. Education as the main character is directly affected and includes many new partners.

The power and potential of corporate training are too often overlooked by people in government, in traditional education, and in industry itself. They simply do not realize its size and impact or they may just consider it another short-cut to greater productivity. But its scope and implications as a major American educational resource are far broader and demand attention and understanding. Corporate education and training programs are, in fact, one of the largest providers of adult education in America.

At first glance, corporate education would seem to be a "private sector" issue, but in reality it is a matter of public policy as well. The "public sector" is paying for corporate education and training because the cost of these programs is defined as a recognized cost of doing business. It is a regular business expense. Some industries and corporations can, under current tax law, write off as much as 50 percent of such costs as essential for productivity. The other 50 percent goes along to the price consumers pay for a product or service. It could be argued, of course, that as efficiency and productivity are improved by better trained or educated employees, the price may be reduced. No matter how it is argued, there are big stakes in corporate education programs and the public foots the bill.

EDUCATION: AN INVESTMENT

Education is as much a business need as running a laboratory or a plant. Gradually, major companies are making human resource investments just as they would make capital investments—in essential education and training that will give employees skills, knowledge and attitudes that will make them more productive and competitive. The education or training deemed "essential" may vary from a few hours' training on a construction site

2

to highly elaborate technological programs to sequential courses designed to foster personal development of top management.

These classrooms should be seen as vital contributors to the array of adult educational opportunities in America. They are an essential national resource, crucial to maintaining and sharpening America's competitive position. Our society cannot evaluate its problems, nor certainly consider solutions, without taking into account a major provider of education for productivity.

If America is to be an effective international competitor, then innovation, vitality, and effective training of the work force are key ingredients. Both corporate education and university-business ties will need to be strengthened. Erich Bloch, former Vice President for Technical Personnel Development at IBM and now Director of the National Science Foundation, is an urgent advocate of this view. He says, "The United States can only remain competitive by addressing two major problem areas: education and research. On neither count is the nation keeping up with its competitors. . . . It is incumbent on industry, together with the academic community, to take the necessary countermeasures."[1]

Education and research reside in people and knowledge. The authors of *Global Stakes* emphasize that *knowledge* has become a strategic resource as vital as natural resources and physical investments. They argue that we must change the way national priorities and strategies are set, and they conclude, "The most important among these propositions concerns education, and the strategic, long-term need to resupport and reorient the American system of education. Another concerns training, and the need to revamp our approach to retraining workers who are displaced by technological change."[2]

The importance of corporation education and the need for a more effective alliance with traditional education to improve the nation's economic performance is not seen by all. In 1984, two prestigious think tanks issued reports on the challenges to American industrial growth. Neither included corporate education as a prominent aspect of the solution. *A Blueprint for Jobs and Industrial Growth*, from The Heritage Foundation, does not relate increased industrial productivity to corporate training, but simply tosses the job of providing an effective work force back to the school system. The report does ask the business community to cooperate with schools and to aid programs like work study, but it points out, too simplistically perhaps, that education is not a "primary mission" in the business community: Education within industry is simply a means to the end of better workers.[3] Yet highly sophisticated technical education as well as broadly conceived general education are being offered in the most successful, larger corporations crucial to U.S. industrial growth.

To Promote Prosperity, from the Hoover Institution, mentions corporate education and training not at all. Here the problems of the work force reside in the public schools with their lowered standards—from discipline to academic requirements to the evaluation of students. The United States needs no additional college education and graduates, says this report. Why educate more when so many college graduates are either unemployed or minimally employed?[4] It is a dismal view for prosperity and ignores what is actually going on on corporate campuses.

Two recent best-selling books on corporate strategies for excellence also neglect corporate education and training. This is a curious oversight because the companies they study have extensive in-house educational commitments. *In Search of Excellence* does not consider corporate education and training. *The 100 Best Companies to Work for in America* does not make education or training one of the criteria for "best" companies.[5] Nevertheless, the highly rated companies do operate strong training and educational programs that workers rightly see as a benefit and an opportunity for advancement. Education may be an important consideration in whether the best recruits decide to work for the company.

SIZE AND SCOPE

Time and time again, whenever America's total educational opportunities and resources are surveyed and evaluated, corporate classrooms are ignored or underplayed. And yet, they have been teaching—in one form or another—since the first Industrial Revolution. Corporate education has grown and flourished behind closed doors; few outsiders have even recognized its existence, much less known about its forms and functions. In fact, those *inside* the classrooms often know little about what is going on

4

in other classrooms within their own or other companies. Why so many shadows around programs that involve millions of Americans and billions of dollars?

One reason for the ignorance is that such programs are frequently decentralized and operate in company branches, units, or satellite firms scattered across the country. Programs have usually developed pragmatically, with courses and training offered as needed at various plant locations. As a result of decentralization and departmental budgeting procedures, most corporations cannot tell you their total costs for education and training. Sometimes education costs are simply chalked up to operating expenses when an employee is assigned to a course that is necessary for his or her performance.

There is also the question of whether companies really want to know the total amount they actually spend on education. If they do, and if they can determine the total, they simply may not want to disclose it to others. On a still more practical level, trainers reporting total education amounts may find themselves confronting a large budget line—an item subject to cuts at belt-tightening time as "luxuries" or inefficiencies; efficient training delivery is an important aspect of corporate education decisions. And, if you do know why announce it?

Further, the cost of educating employees may be an insignificant item when the corporation's budget may be in the billions of dollars. Also setting up a standard format for collecting and using cost data for education programs is a complicated matter. In fact, one study found that "on average, administrators were able to report only slightly more than half of the 'full' costs uncovered."[6]

Thus, even though the corporate classroom is a major and increasingly important source of adult learning in the United States, it is possible to make only rough, very rough, estimates of its total size in terms of costs, programs and numbers of employee-students. Such estimates vary widely—some would say, wildly—and estimates depend of course on what is being counted. The biggest question in costing corporate education is: Do you count student-employee wages and benefits during the training period? Obviously, this is a very large item and yet it is seldom recognized in analyses and evaluations.

5

Education expenditure is usually figured on instructor cost, course development, tuition and facility cost, not employee-student time and wages. Further, on-the-job training is rarely included in totals because it is an ongoing process, difficult to break out in such factors as supervisor's time, colleague's demonstration time, and so forth. Therefore, the base for measuring is generally the "formal" scheduled education cost, with a lot of informal education left uncounted.

For all of these reasons, estimates of corporate expenditure on education lack reliability. Estimates range from a relatively conservative low of $40 billion spent annually by private sector employers only to an apparently extravagant high of $100 billion spent by both public and private sector employers. Thomas F. Gilbert defended his higher estimate, based on 1975 data, saying it was not a "whimsical public relations figure," but that it *did* include estimates for employee wages and benefits as well as public funds spent by local, state, and federal governments for employee training—approximately $10 billion. Gilbert did not, however, include on-the-job training. That, he points out, would offset estimates of scheduled costs.[7]

Several studies suggest that direct, scheduled training costs would at least double if employees' compensation figures for training time were included. And corporate officers agree. On this basis, taking the estimate of $40 billion made by the American Society for Training and Development, the total would reach $80 billion with wages included—and that estimate was made several years ago with no inflation factor figured.

Even when the salaries and wages paid during training are omitted for purposes of comparison with higher education costs, it appears that private corporations may be approaching the total amount spent annually by our nation's universities and other four-year colleges, both public and private. That figure for 1981-1982—the latest figure available—was just over $60 billion.

Harold Hodgkinson, formerly Director of the National Institute of Education and of the Professional Institute of the American Management Associations, suggested in 1981 that the "size and value were coming close to the net worth of the 3,500 colleges and universities whose total investment is about $55 billion."[8] In the same year, the Center for Public

6

Resources that works closely with industry estimated $60 billion as "about what business spends annually on in-house and company sponsored education."[9] Whatever the exact amount, private employers are running a massive program.

On the other hand, measuring the size of industry-sponsored education by the number of workers receiving it does not yield firm figures either. Estimates of employees receiving education and training (based on the Bureau of the Census Current Population Survey) are notoriously low due to the data collection method, the ways in which questions are asked and the respondent's accuracy and understanding of what was meant by a "course." It has been found that workers surveyed report taking longer, formal courses while overlooking the short training sessions they may have had.

Worker survey data, for example, reveal only one-third as much training within government agencies as the agencies themselves report. And agency data reporting itself is seen by most observers as understated to begin with.[10] Similarly, another review of adult education statistics gathered in the Population Survey for many types of institutions (including government and industry) concludes that "only roughly half of all courses or training activities were reported."[11]

Harold Goldstein, a former Labor Department economist and authority on both the Population Survey and on industry training data, hazards the guess that in 1978 business firms gave in-house training to about 6.8 million trainees, and the number of courses taken would be somewhat higher—8 million—if one uses the ratio of courses to participants given in the survey.[12]

In 1981, procedures were changed for the Population Survey and interviewers made a second household visit, if necessary, to talk with training participants themselves and thus obtain more complete information. Results revealed a dramatic increase over the three-year period. The number of employee education courses provided by business firms increased by 62 percent, while total wage and salary employment in the firms grew by only 6 percent.[13] The reporting process was improved, of course, but results still suggest significant growth in the numbers of courses industry sponsored.

Despite the difficulties and inaccuracies of obtaining and reporting data, there is no question that many millions of adults are learning a wide variety of skills in corporate classrooms. Without undue exaggeration, the figure may well reach the total enrollment of 7,654,000 in America's public and private four-year colleges and universities in 1982.

More precise data on corporate classroom activities and costs emerge by studying particular companies. A look at two giants in the corporate world reveals how vast the larger programs have become. AT&T, before divestiture of local companies in 1984, had nearly one million employees, about 1 percent of *all* American workers, and reportedly spent $1.7 billion for employee training in 1980. The corporation conducted some 12,000 courses in 1,300 locations for 20,000 to 30,000 employees per day with 13,000 trainers and support staff.[14] Robert Craig, formerly of the American Society for Training and Development, updated the Bell System's total educational costs as approaching $2 billion for 1982.

An analysis of AT&T's 1977 figures showed their expenditure hitting $700 million—and compared it to the $222 million budget of the Massachusetts Institute of Technology for the same year. Stan Luxenberg concluded the analysis simply, "AT&T performs more education and training functions than any university in the world."[15] It should be noted that in the five years since Luxenberg's study, AT&T had more than doubled its education and training budget. As a regulated utility held responsible for accounting and controlling its costs, AT&T has been a leader in efforts to standardize a system for collecting training data.

Another corporate giant, IBM, in 1982 invested more than $500 million in education for their employees, who numbered 215,000 in the United States and 150,000 abroad.[16] And by 1984 a corporate vice president thought $700 million a reasonably adequate guess. IBM has recognized since the 1940s the vital importance of training their new employees with care and then supporting their career development with broad educational opportunities. IBM's leadership notably comes from within the ranks; employee education is an investment in the future of both the individual and the corporation. In a high-tech firm such as IBM it is crucial to be up-to-date, and both technical professionals and managers are required to take at least 40 hours of instruction each year.

But, in view of the size of corporate education, an obvious and immediate question is: How do employer-sponsored training and education programs weather changes in the overall economic climate? Cutbacks, it seems, are not as widespread as one might guess. One survey found that despite the recession, 1982 was generally characterized by growth and budget increases or by maintenance of existing programs. Training executives were generally optimistic about 1983, but a follow-up survey found the projections to be too optimistic: actual budgets tended to be more static.[17]

Another 1982 survey, however, found 1983 projections, in gross terms, somewhat pessimistic. Responses reflected anticipation of static or decreasing budgets for smaller companies, while for larger companies slightly more than half responding predicted increased budgets.[18] Economic ups and downs hit corporate education activities, but primarily only to slow growth or maintain the status quo.

Larger corporations, as would be expected, have developed more in-house as well as more extensive educational programs than have smaller companies. Corporations with less than 500 employees usually have part-time training programs and use more outside assistance or make cooperative arrangements with local educational institutions, particularly community colleges, for training purposes. Many smaller businesses offer no employer-sponsored education, and it is well to remember that 51 percent of workers are in companies employing 100 or less people. Clearly, corporate education is unevenly distributed.

This study naturally concentrates on large corporations because that is where the action is. Classroom examples come primarily from the *Fortune 500* companies. Many are multinational corporations; their education and training programs are exported to large numbers of employees and customers; they create global classrooms. And corporation trainers are teaching the citizens of other countries in a new kind of universal education.

Further differences exist among types of industries; some require more constant education and reeducation than others. For example, banking and insurance firms have their own long histories in education and well-established programs located in every large population center. Public utilities also have, for years, ranked high in the amount of training given supervisors and executives as well as professional and technical personnel. Industrial manufacturing firms are high on training, while transportation companies—with the exception of the airlines—have generally not reported such sizeable programs. In the fields of merchandising and retail sales, training has not received great attention, but now some have established impressive training centers like McDonald's Hamburger University and Holiday Inn University.

Another distinction in the nature of companies that offer more or less education was made in a prescient statement in 1966 by Charles DeCarlo and Ormsbee Robinson in their forward-looking book, *Education in Business and Industry*. Commenting on the modern corporation's increasing dependence upon technological investment and emphasis on research and development (R&D), they concluded that:

> The most advanced education programs are found in those industries which have the highest investment in R&D. . . . If R&D is considered an index of technological activity and the causative agent in developing requirements for education and training programs, then the number of R&D scientists employed per total number of employees in a given company will be related to that company's requirements for education and training investment.[19]

With advancing technology—the new devices and processes created by R&D—manufacturing procedures change and necessitate worker training. These changes radiate through sales and management functions. Drawing from data compiled by the National Science Foundation, the authors found the heaviest concentration of scientists and engineers in: aircraft and missiles, scientific and mechanical measuring instruments, communications equipment and electronic components, electrical equipment, and drugs and medicine. And they further state that "R&D investment and manpower development seem to go hand in hand with satisfactory levels of growth and employment."

10

Their observations were made almost two decades ago, and everything found in this current study supports the conclusion. Today's larger high-tech firms—with their essential emphasis on R&D—are centers for the most active and innovative education and training programs, many of them directed toward constant training of their own scientists and engineers.

It is no surprise, therefore, that IBM, which spends some $3 billion a year on research, development and engineering, insures and enhances that investment with its *own* extensive education and training program. Nor is it extraordinary that Hewlett-Packard plowed back 10 percent on sales of $4 billion in 1981 for R&D, and supports that $400 million investment with a far-reaching and enlightened corporate educational system. Similar development philosophies are found at Texas Instruments, Digital Equipment Corporation, Control Data, Wang, and others. Erik Jonsson, one of the founders of Texas Instruments, says that he wants the corporation to have the equivalent of its own "internal university." Given the multitude of educational opportunities offered employees at every level, there is little doubt that TI in effect already has its private university.

Literally millions of new jobs have been created in America because of high technology and its applications. People are either working at new jobs or they are working in entirely new industries. Technologically-intensive industry has been growing much faster than other industries, and employment in high-tech applications is growing even faster. New jobs are appearing in computer sciences to develop machines, to service the machines, to create software. And every industry from banking to utilities to sales will require men and women who are technologically up-to-date. High-tech products, with their limited life spans, compel continuing education of workers in every category as ever more subtle and adjustable machines are introduced.

But high tech, as influential as it is in spawning new demands for training, tells only the glamorous front page of the whole corporate education story. To reveal the larger pattern of industrial education generally, references here draw on a wider sample of corporations and include natural resource companies, public utilities, the automotive industry, financial services like banking and insurance, publishing, and merchandising.

11

Comprehensive education as it is delivered by the nation's colleges and schools is not the *first* business of business today, but in the more advanced companies such education is expanding. Corporate classrooms are teaching more subjects customarily found in traditional education even though their purposes differ.

REASONS FOR CORPORATE TRAINING

Why are corporations choosing to develop their own expensive and extensive education system? Beyond the obvious fact that you can't stay in business long with pockets of ignorance throughout the plant, there is the question of broadening the subject matter deemed necessary for many personnel and which the companies themselves have decided to teach. From the corporate viewpoint there are ample reasons:

Compensatory education is needed on both basic and advanced professional levels. Employment of minorities, immigrants, and school dropouts—as well as those poorly trained from schools—necessitates remedial courses in reading, writing, and arithmetic. On higher levels, advanced engineering has also been required since machines entered the workplace and started a continuing "revolution" that moves faster and faster. Twenty years ago it was observed that the newly graduated engineer was already behind because his textbooks were outdated. So, for many years, technical progress for a company has depended on continual upgrading of its scientific personnel.

Today this also means managers must understand technological advances that revolutionize the processes they command. Organizational theory and case studies that managers once had in business schools are outdated too. Compensatory education in this broader sense—required by the advancement in knowledge and its applications—is a vital obligation if the company is to stay in business.

Company-oriented education is equally vital to survival. From the introduction of the new employee to the mysterious ways of the particular corporate culture to the highest executives' sessions on strategic planning and decision-making, the company must indoctrinate its own and build

12

its corporate structure. Such orientation is not done by osmosis, but by well-conceived schemes of training and development that accompany the employee's career. From the first supervisory promotion to the top echelon, he or she receives training both in skills for working with people and in the ways and procedures of Company X.

In-house education also improves cooperation and communication among employees. After studying together for a week or two of intensive training, perhaps on a secluded corporate campus, fellow workers are more apt to consult each other in the future on decisions affecting more than their own part of the company. The corporate table of organization has taken on faces and personalities, and loyalties frequently form stronger networks than the chart's dotted lines of control.

Employees in sales get continuing company-specific and essential education for every new product appearing. With intense competition, some companies are jumping to satellite instruction to reach their sales and service personnel more quickly. One leader in the high-tech field, for example, estimates an edge, via satellite communications, of three to four months in reaching the marketplace. In every large company, product sales and services are the bottom line, and extensive training efforts go directly there. It is also where one finds courses in ethics to guide salesmanship. More responsible companies—looking ahead to long-range effects—insist on careful explanation of the product's effectiveness and where it is *not* effective. It is myopic to make the sale and lose the customer.

Recruitment and employee benefits are enhanced by educational opportunities. Because they see more college graduates in the labor force and recognize that education begets education, corporations are providing more of it and more choices—including courses eligible for academic credit at traditional educational institutions and advanced degree work paid for by the company. Reports indicate that direct pressure from employees and potential recruits, particularly for technical positions, further drives the demand for training programs.

In some instances, company rationale is to discourage unionization and keep an open shop; this is a frankly stated reason. In other cases, where the company is already unionized, labor unions argue for contractual educational benefits. Not long ago AT&T, well-known for its enlightened education program, found itself negotiating an additional $31 million for retraining employees in new technologies. Labor's spokesmen said it "would help cushion . . . lay offs and job changes: . . . We have moved ahead toward providing career development opportunities for our members in this volatile information age."[20] Training has become a negotiable item for labor contracts in several large industries.

For many reasons, companies are in the education business. Federal regulations such as affirmative action mandates and the Occupational Safety and Health Act dictate specific training for special purposes. In other instances, companies offer more general courses for *individual* development and advancement. Company catalogs increasingly list training courses for personal growth and satisfaction that enhance the quality of life. It is a cue to motivation, another key to productivity that opens classroom doors. Trends are away from mass-oriented programs; movement is toward encouraging individual development on company time.

CORPORATE CLASSROOMS AND HIGHER EDUCATION

While some company needs can be met through cooperative arrangements with colleges and universities, and others through consultants and vendors of packaged training materials, on the whole, corporations provide for themselves with their own trainers. Estimates are that from 60 to 80 percent of corporate education and training is in house. Businesses can do it their own way for their own purposes. They have more flexibility in content, time elements, method of presentation, and in making changes as desired. Costs are apt to be less. The teacher is their own employee who works conventional business hours and brings practical experience into the classroom. Indications mark not only the continuance of in-house education but suggest its growth.

And this may well be for the best, if not inevitable, because industrial education and the traditional system have evolved to accomplish important but different missions. The goal of traditional higher education is, and must be, broader: it seeks to teach concepts and their evolution, critical methods of inquiry and knowledge in various subjects, historical background as well as current issues, and provide the bases for many professions taught at advanced levels. In comparison, the corporate system's goal is more specific and narrow in terms of applicability to a company's needs and productivity. The overlap, however, is growing as corporations realize that continual learning for workers in a variety of fields may actively improve production.

The differences in goals between industry's program and the traditional system should not imply that one is "training" and the other "education." Purists like to make this distinction, but as Patricia Cross points out, it is a difference that is difficult and superficial to maintain:

> Non-collegiate organizations have moved into "education" almost as fast as colleges, especially community colleges, have moved into "training," and the distinction is now blurred beyond usefulness—at least when applied to providers. Colleges are heavily involved in training as well as in education; and the programs of many corporations contain as much emphasis on theory, research, and personal development as any business school.[21]

One is reminded of common usage as well in referring to medical training or education. Hence, in this study the words are used interchangeably for convenience.

Differences in mission between the two systems have led, however, to marked contrast in styles that hamper cooperation. Higher education enjoys a more leisurely and wider time frame with such traditional academic routines as 50-minute class hours three times a week. Some say the routines are hardened, rigid, and encrusted to their own detriment.[22] To the corporate world, with its pattern of short-term, intensive hours, and highly motivated employee-students, academia appears luxurious. In their world, "time frames" are costly and company controls well understood.

Frequently, starting from opposite poles, cooperation has proved to be neither feasible nor desirable—certainly not mutually satisfactory. It has engendered distrust and discomfort, if not disdain; it has often been abandoned as not worth the effort on either side.

15

Where collaboration has worked, it has been on a limited basis for fairly specific purposes, and it has been guided by cooperative individuals who build effective personal relationships. Planning collaborative programs with particular segments of higher education like business schools and engineering departments works, because there are logical connections and obvious needs.

Cooperative programs also have a high success record on local and limited regional levels, and they are especially consistent with the foremost purpose of community colleges: to serve community needs. They are conveniently located for area industries and small businesses with specific requirements. For years, programs like those in Miami-Dade County, Chicago's and Los Angeles' community colleges, and New York's LaGuardia Community College have served well.

Through national associations the 1,274 community colleges in the country are building networks of alliance with business. General Motors Corporation, for example, has contracts with about 45 community colleges around the country to train service technicians for its automobile dealerships; G.M. in turn trains the schools' faculty members. Linkages are extending to match better the skills of workers entering the job market with industries' needs.

Between 1980 and 1982 the American Association of Community and Junior Colleges and the Small Business Training Network linked 186 two-year colleges to district offices of the U.S. Small Business Administration to organize and deliver more than two million hours of short-term training in 47 states.[23] Cooperation works for this segment of higher education and for vocational and technical institutes, but frequently with the handicaps of obsolete equipment and obsolete faculty who lack direct access to the latest techniques and developments in industry, which has always and naturally been ahead of classroom teachers.

Similarly, the natural affinity between universities' schools of business with MBA courses and management needs of the corporate world has led to successful higher education-industry connections. The mission of business schools and their long history of development to provide for executive needs have created an alliance that serves both as a recruitment source for corporations and a center for retraining executives. It now appears,

16

however, that more corporations are developing their own upper-level management courses with specific corporate orientation and subscribing less generally to what some corporate leaders criticize as the too theoretical approach of business schools. So, even with their strong symbiotic relationship built over many years, business schools, too, need change and a more pragmatic approach to satisfy many corporations.

Engineering schools also have had their direct pipeline to industry; that was their mission and they have fulfilled it well—perhaps too well in view of the fact that industry's almost insatiable demand for engineers and ability to pay high salaries have robbed them of much needed faculty. Because of recent attention and current emphasis on the United States' precarious position in competitive world markets, this imbalance is recognized and corrective action is under way.

Many new and stronger links are being forged, especially with technological corporations, and initiative is coming from both sides. IBM and others offer top technical personnel to teach; exchanges are set; Seattle University's School of Engineering has started, with assistance from Boeing, a new master's degree for software engineering to accommodate Boeing employees as well as other students. Wang's leadership inaugurated an independent graduate institute to meet industry's need in this same area.

Fifteen prestigious universities from the Association for Media-Based Continuing Education for Engineers—together with 12 leading corporations—have started the new National Technological University, operating via satellite to reach engineers in corporate classrooms for advanced professional work leading to NTU's master of science degree. Details are given in Chapter V. A bold and potentially very large venture, NTU's delivery system takes high quality instruction from major universities to the workplace.

It is one answer to the main recommendations in MIT's comprehensive report on *Lifelong Cooperative Education* for engineers. Questioning the basic assumption that a few years' formal education can prove adequate for a lifetime in professional engineering, and recognizing the urgency and need for improvement that arise from the rapid growth of knowledge-intensive industry, the MIT report calls for:

- close collaboration between engineering faculties and their industrial colleagues, including the use of industrial experts in designing specialized courses;
- opening engineering schools to employed engineers for part-time study and, in reverse, more arrangements like Stanford's to take classes by instructional television into the region's industries;
- corporate executives to support formal study for engineers of all ages "whether working at the bench or managing large projects." Demands cannot be met by replacing "obsolescent engineers with new graduates," and even if they could, the human costs would be unacceptable.[24]

In summary, the far-reaching report asks for teamwork by engineering schools, industry, and professional societies to provide continual education for engineers. Many gaps that separate "work" and "study" must be bridged for the benefit of all concerned. The coalition of industry, engineering schools, and professional societies starts from strong and deep roots. With leadership it can become a model for other practicing professionals needing more opportunities for continuing education.

On another vital front—collaborative scientific research between universities and corporations—arrangements are appearing at an astonishing rate. Both parties seem able and eager to cope with the obvious and inherent difficulties such projects pose when financial stakes are high and the chance to advance human knowledge is the challenge. Carefully drawn contracts that protect academic freedom in research and the open availability of results seem feasible, but it is still early to predict success. Professors involved often have two masters and sometimes two workplaces. Nevertheless, research collaboration can be a beneficial relationship for both parties.

Major universities' research centers and corporations have entered into such arrangements in significant numbers and for large dollar amounts. Universities whose research funds have been sharply curtailed by federal government policies welcome support. And the discovery of "truth"—or even new facts—is part of their function. Corporations, correspondingly, have a chance at additional creative breakthroughs that may yield prof-

18

itable new products and processes. There are shared risks and shared advantages.

In each of these examples from community colleges, business schools, departments of engineering, and research laboratories, cooperative programs are fairly specific and consistent with at least part of the mission of traditional education, and they answer a definite need on the corporate side.

CORPORATE SUPPORT FOR EDUCATION

On a larger scale, relationships between business and traditional education become more diffuse and general but nonetheless real, especially in the matter of financial support for higher education. Both in direct grants and tuition refund plans, corporations have long been contributors. In the last four years, corporations have increased gifts to education by 46 percent despite the uncertain economic climate in which profits declined. Corporate gifts totaled $1.29 billion for 1983, an all time high and testimony to their commitment to education.[25]

Some 80–90 percent of corporations have well-established tuition refund policies for employees to study in colleges and other higher education institutions. While such policies are certainly constructive, particularly so in an era of declining enrollment and shrinking income, only about 5 to 7 percent of eligible employees took advantage of the opportunity up to 1979 when the tax law was changed. There had been confusion over issues/ of job-relatedness and whether tuition aid was taxable as employee income. Since the 1979 ruling, the percentage of workers participating is said to have nearly doubled, and the participation of lower paid workers has especially grown.

Lately, corporate gifts of equipment, with tax incentive, have also caught public attention, particularly in the competition for the computer market on collegiate campuses. Beginning with institutions known primarily for their science and technology education, computers and varieties of electronic equipment have gone to Princeton, Bucknell and many other institutions. Such gifts help to bridge gaps of obsolescence and bring higher education closer to the "cutting edge" of industry.

19

Still, with all these cooperative and supportive efforts, industry remains obliged to provide for its own first needs; it has never been able to rely on the traditional system with its various and different goals and styles. If it had, the United States would probably never have achieved its economic preeminence. Without corporate education, the nation will not compete successfully in the future. Industry has, nevertheless, received its basic educational underpinning and certain types of specialized skills from the established system.

ADULT LEARNING RESOURCES

Corporate sector education has been called a "shadow" system and a "second" system, but such labels are both misleading and questionable. It is not a shadow and it is second to none in the integrity of its programs and purposes. The corporate system is educating many millions of adults in this nation. Its classrooms are more than the primary center for improving human resources to enhance productivity; they are a major center for adult education, a leading contributor to America's total learning opportunities.

Today the notion of lifelong education has become a public and private goal and a necessity. More than an ideal, it is entrenched in the American way of life to a remarkable extent unmatched in other nations. More than 21 million people, almost 13 percent of the total adult U.S. population, are taking courses that are "organized" educationally, and they are studying on a part-time basis.[26] Estimates for course-taking in *nonschool* settings like churches and synagogues, government services, professional associations, and agricultural extension reach as high as 46 million.[27] Who knows how many take courses on television and through other forms of independent study? Figures are slippery and definitions of "courses" not too clear; but one thing is clear: lots of adults are continuing to learn.

Adult education is the only part of the American educational world that is growing, in part because of shifts in the population. Those 65 and over are increasing at twice the rate of the national population, just over a 67 percent increase since 1960. They are, more than ever before, using their leisure and retirement for educational activities. Of most significance

20

for the work force and productivity, however, is the spectacular growth—48 percent—in this age group (18-64) because of the maturing of the postwar, baby-boom generation. There are now 146 million in this age category that continues to grow.

Concurrently, the college population has been shrinking and will continue to do so for some years. Not until 1995 is traditional higher education enrollment expected to rise again. And, with more people finding it wise and convenient to attend school at different periods in life, the establishment is changing. Many more part-time students and adults at advancing age levels attend. Colleges and universities have a greater mix in ages.

Looking at the providers for total adult education reveals that two-year colleges and technical institutes and four-year colleges and universities together comprise the greatest source for continuing students. Each group offers slightly more than seven million courses taken by adult learners. Business and industry ranks next as educational provider in the United States. To evaluate the corporations' role, however, it must be noted that they *paid* for over 12 million courses while individuals or families paid for 17 million.

What are people studying and why? Most courses are taken for job-related reasons, especially to improve current positions or to advance, but a large number are not related to employment. Many are enrolled for general education, personal and social reasons that lead them to study particularly in established institutions. As to subjects studied, business not unexpectedly is the winner with eight and a half million courses taken; health care with health sciences shows nearly four million, while engineering and technology course registration is just over three and one half million.

The largest group of adult students are professional and technical workers, clerical workers are next, and managers and administrators are third in the number of courses for which they are enrolled.

But corporate classrooms obviously have first access to the working-age population, the group that has grown significantly and is the most crucial to our nation's economy and position in worldwide competition.

To the extent that the corporation gives training or pays for it elsewhere, it is vital to the country's needs and decisive to the economic outcome.

Not only have corporations inherited the results of the postwar baby-boom, they have also inherited the results of the education boom of the 1960s and early '70s. Never before have so many college graduates been in the work force. Nearly 25 percent of all workers have completed college, and degree-holding workers will represent a growing proportion of the labor force for the rest of the 1980s because more than a million men and women annually will obtain some advanced degree. About 43 percent of the entire American work force has at least a high school diploma. This immediately affects corporate policy and what goes on in corporate classrooms. Those with education are apt to expect and want more, which is evident in adult course enrollment.

Education and training are an absolute necessity in the world of work—an integral part of progress—just as they were after the first Industrial Revolution of the nineteenth century. Only now the pace has quickened. Manufacturing processes are moving into a new phase technologically controlled, and robotics are coming into position; communications will create jobs still only imaginable; service industries—nonmaterial consumables—are expanding to care for all sorts of human needs; health services and care are rapidly expanding. The computer worlds with their networks, biotechnology, and aerospace development all challenge the working world to keep up.

Mismatches between industry's needs and higher education's products are inevitable. The gap has always existed, but now it seems to widen more rapidly as laboratories hum around the clock on Route 128 in Massachusetts and in Silicon Valley in California. Although many entrepreneurs meet failure, new announcements continue.

Large corporations, and particularly those on the high-tech front, are pouring time and money into keeping their personnel abreast of developments or, better yet, ahead. Their classrooms provide learning for the millions of adults who will change jobs or tasks four to five times in their work lives. Hence, any view of educational opportunities for adults in our society that does not include the corporate educational system is missing a major sector where countless numbers are learning.

22

A national education policy is urgently needed to strengthen America's competitive position in the world. Business and higher education leaders together are pleading for a comprehensive approach. All human resources must be examined and utilized for effective action. A new look is essential, one that joins the strengths of collegiate and corporate education while respecting the different purposes and missions of the two systems.

The United States Congress—not noted for its timely action except under national duress—voted the Higher Education Act in 1972 with the words: "The American people need lifelong learning to enable them to adjust to social, technological, political, and economic changes." No significant financial or detailed program accompanied the legislation that declared a new national vision for adult learning. But neither did a detailed program accompany the pronouncement made by John Gardiner, the orator who acclaimed America's pragmatism 200 years ago.

CHAPTER II

Training Workers: A Backward Glance

"IN NO PART of the habitable globe is learning and true *useful* knowledge so universally disseminated," orator John Gardiner joyously proclaimed to a Boston audience on July 4, 1785. America harkened to the whirring and clattering of the Industrial Revolution and eagerly pursued the promise of prosperity through power-driven machinery, steam engines and a factory system that put useful knowledge and new technology to productive ends.

Rapid, innovative, and competitive manufacturing was seen as vital to the agrarian society rich in natural resources but heretofore cut off from English industrialization by pre-Revolutionary restrictive trade and production regulations. By 1787 John Fitch's steamboat had made its successful trip on the Delaware River. Slater's spinning mill was in operation in Rhode Island by 1791. Eli Whitney's cotton gin came in 1793 and, in 1798, David Wilkinson patented a machine for making other machines. Thousands of mechanical inventions, major and minor, had been put to industrial use by 1850. Technological advancement—the alteration of tools and other material used to perform work—meant that the nature of work and workers was fundamentally changed. This early American drive for industrialization was so successful that, for example, in 1807 there were 15 cotton mills in the country, and by 1815 mills utilizing 500,000 spindles were employing 76,000 workers. These men, women, and children were already being called "industrial workers."

TRANSFORMING A PEOPLE

But there were not enough industrial workers to meet the new demands. Early in the nineteenth century, inventor Eli Whitney's Interchangeable

System for mass production was an essential development, he claimed, to "substitute correct and effective operations of machinery for . . . a species of skill which is not possessed in this country to any considerable extent."[1] America was not a nation of mechanics; it was a nation of farmers and craftsmen in the midst of an utter transformation of society.

Industrialization meant two changes in work preparation. Specific training was now required before specific tasks could be performed. In the traditional craft and agrarian order, people had "grown-up" into stable, life-long occupations. The other change required a different orientation: Work activity was now focused away from the individual, family, or small group and toward a large, impersonal organization within a large, impersonal urban community. The Industrial Revolution required education for specific tasks *and* education to function within the emerging corporate organization.[2]

Early American values and the phenomenal social changes wrought by industrialization combined to instill in people a sense of personal freedom and a happy vigilance for the accidents of opportunity. There was a generally shared vision of this new institution—the factory system—as itself a primary means for uplifting the masses. Factory work was to be a step along life's way, not life's work. There was little, if any, thought of creating the permanent industrial laboring class that came later with its problems. American entrepreneurs of the first decades were genuinely distressed by images of the physically degraded and mentally defeated industrial labor force of England. These men took themselves seriously as businessmen, employers, and as agents for human enlightenment.

A major impediment to industrial progress was the labor shortage. The apprenticeship system had been for centuries the primary means of training for a trade. It involved, however, a commitment of years and imposed obligations and burdens on both employer and employee. The system had never been very practicable in colonial America. And with the new democratic impulse and the Industrial Revolution's demands, apprenticeship proved inadequate as an efficient source of labor, although in the very early days it provided temporarily a source of cheap labor. Workers' groups soon set out to inhibit apprenticeship in factories and, in a way, resist technology. Philadelphia hatters, for example, wrote a stringent code for themselves: One apprentice only to a shop and expulsion for any member who worked with any labor-saving apparatus. Other early workers' groups restricted apprenticeship.[3] At the same time, independent adult male labor was very scarce; able-bodied men were primarily on farms or involved in the shipping trade.

Another approach to provide labor was the family scheme. Some manufacturers brought entire families from the New England countryside and organized factory communities with positions for men, women and children. The rural character of this labor force helped shape employer-employee relations. One particularly ambitious attempt to establish an industrial operating environment reflects the early idealistic development in corporate life. In 1806 the Pomfret Manufacturing Company bought 1,000 acres of land in Windham County, Connecticut, and put up the state's first cotton mill. The large land holding was carefully used to create a wholesome factory environment. The company banned taverns from its vicinity. It erected a school and a church. Employee housing was built, and farm work was offered to parents of child mill hands. The scheme attracted wide and favorable attention; public leaders made special note of this fine American contrast to the despised English industrial system. The once prosperous Pomfret mills and some 15 millworkers' dwellings still stand.[4] The family scheme did not work at many factories, however, and as it degenerated to outright exploitation in industrial centers, it was rejected by manufacturers and labor alike.

The bulk of the factory labor force would be young women from New England's farms. Massachusetts manufacturers, recruiting maidens to tend spindles at the great mills of Lowell, Lawrence, and other manufacturing centers, provided not just a job but an entire set of living circumstances designed to nurture and educate. Here the boardinghouse system was born. "The idea behind Lowell," Foster Rhea Dulles concluded in his study of American labor history, "was virtually that of a female boarding school, except that the young women worked in the mills rather than at their studies."[5]

Around the big brick mills, owners maintained rambling boarding houses where the girls lived, supervised by a matron and with such amenities as upright pianos. Literary evenings, elevating lectures, and

27

circulating libraries were available. A magazine was published in Lowell and subsidized at least in part by manufacturers; the *Lowell Offering* was entirely made up of stories and articles by factory operatives. Girls lives were under the control of mill owners. Church attendance was expected, with manufacturers building the church and the girls paying the pew fee.[6] Immodesty, profanity, dancing, or more serious lapses were all grounds for dismissal. Boarding house doors closed at 10 p.m. Girls could save money if they were careful—they were paid a handsome $3.00 a week for working 13 hours a day, six days a week. About a dollar went to board.[7]

Male workers also labored under the strict eye of the mill owners, particularly regarding morals, health and well-being. The giant Lowell Manufacturing Company explicitly stated that it would not "continue to employ any person who shall be wanting in proper respects to the females employed by the company, or who shall smoke within the company's premises, or be guilty of inebriety."[8]

While the manufacturer's concern for the total life of workers during these early years is impressive, it is even more so when we remember that these were not small operations. The Merrimack Manufacturing Company in Lowell, for example, had 1,000 looms in 1833, employed 400 males and 900 females, and produced an annual average of 6,500,000 yards of finished cloth. Lowell mills were producing cloth at the rate of one yard per second in the early 1830s and required so much new labor that some 25 boarding houses a month were being built.[9]

A letter written in 1840 from one of the boarding houses of the Lawrence mills reflects the brighter side of industrialization that characterized the early factory life. "Dear Mamma," Miss Jerusha Holbrook wrote, "The Mill owners here are the kindest men imaginable. All us employees [sic] are encouraged to read the Bible and the North American Review, which has some very fine thoughts expressed in elegant language; and those girls who are derelict in the attendance at Sabbath School are called upon gently and chided seriously by our Mill overseers, all good Christian men who are also our Teachers on the Sabbath."[10]

Manufacturing advocates were quick to emphasize the superiority of urban and factory living and the advantages that the old, relatively isolated farmer or artisan lacked. There were newspapers, lectures, opportunities for self-improvement. All of these civilizing and enriching factors would, the thinking went, offer food for thought and cultivated discussion during the long, otherwise mindless work hours. The work was not as oppressive then as it might sound, however, and tending spindles was not as hard as factory work would become in later years of industrialization. The girls of the Massachusetts mills found ample time to rest, to read, to talk among themselves, and tend the plants on the factory windowsills. There was a time when the bank deposits of Lowell factory girls averaged as much as $500 each.[11]

One Amasa Walker was an avid early spokesman for the happy and healthy factory life of the modern manufacturing system and laissez-faire economics. Because he feared that the division of labor in factory life— the repetitious performance of a task—tended to "enervate the laborer" he advocated something he called "sanitary arts." These included organized gymnastic exercises and play at the "manly" sports. Physical hygiene and other basics for healthful living should be part of the worker's training, he argued.[12]

Industry became employer, guardian, patron of body and soul. Industries' leaders quickly grasped the utility of these notions, which they did, on the whole, support as useful for promoting industrialization. This willingness to become involved in broad issues of education and quality of life met with a willingness to learn. The new "working class" wanted the opportunities industry offered as much as industry wanted workers with a certain level of intelligence, skill and resourcefulness. These were times filled with new hopes for human welfare, social mobility and economic potential. The new system of manufacture meant that machines were skilled, not men. Craftsmanship belonged to the past, industrial education to the future.

There was no American system of public education to provide "useful knowledge" for potential young workers in the early days of the Industrial Revolution. Training had to be within a company or a trade group and such programs were hardly just lofty exercises in benevolence and self-improvement. They were an absolute necessity. Industries, such as the Lowell mills, wanted a certain type of worker and they created circumstances that would ensure that they got that type of employee. Specialized workers' groups wanted a particular quality of employment and they took similar steps on their own behalf.

The Mechanics Institute was a workers' group in Boston that took one approach to the problem of education for industrial requirements. It established courses and libraries for mechanics and apprentices, but these were limited to men already sufficiently skilled to be in the trade. Other groups sponsored basic education for aspiring mechanics. Such groups drew inspiration from a Scotsman, Dr. George B. Birbeck, who had pioneered British worker education. He believed that scientific education would give workers "an understanding of the principles which underlay their work—an understanding which would elevate manual occupations, so that workers would find fuller satisfaction in their labors and the work itself would be improved."[13]

The Franklin Institute in Philadelphia was an early and important industrial education effort that gave the enthusiasms of early American idealism to this mechanics' movement. It was organized in 1825 by Samuel Merrick, a simple young man whose sudden inheritance made him an entrepreneur. He was shocked to realize, from the height of his new role, the low status of "mere mechanics" in a democratic society. He was disturbed by the difficulties young men faced in obtaining an education in the mechanical arts. His Franklin Institute was organized to teach the principles of science to mechanics and to encourage inventions and manufacturing improvements. It had a library, published a journal, and offered prizes for mechanical inventions. Merrick's abiding faith was that scientific education would enhance both individual opportunity and national industrial progress.

Despite such efforts, workers and industrialists still faced an educational resource crisis. Mechanics institutes were good efforts aimed at the ideal of the generally intelligent, literate and adaptable worker, but they were scarcely adequate to meet demands.

THE RISE OF PUBLIC EDUCATION FOR WORK

Industrial education was summoned as a strong argument for good free public schools. Educational philosophers, social reformers and workers' groups battling for their diverse goals agreed: the multiplying factories with their increasing technology needed workers with greater knowledge and skill, and workers with that education would be in a better position to deal with an increasingly oppressive factory system. Public education must, they urged, prepare citizens by teaching the elements of the mechanical arts and natural sciences needed to earn a productive living in industry or agriculture, the two viable occupational options for the masses. Education could serve both the practical and the enlightened. It could give workers a sense of values and a strong grounding in applied skills. It offered protection from the changing winds of fortune. Universal education could counter oppression at work, enlarge opportunity.

"Its general purpose," said Horace Mann, the indefatigable advocate of free public education, "is to preserve the good and to repudiate the evil which now exists, and to give scope to the sublime law of progression."[14] Mann often based his carefully constructed arguments for schools on their importance in industrializing America. Campaigning in Massachusetts, he was quick to praise the Massachusetts textile manufacturers for their system of boarding houses and elevated evenings. The improvement of manufacture has just begun, he argued, and with educated working men and women the prosperity so long promised would be within reach.

Such arguments appealed in an era when Horace Greeley's image of the "self-made man" was taking hold of the public imagination. After all, in 1848, while these debates raged, a 13-year-old Scottish immigrant named Andrew Carnegie was working 12 hours a day in a Pennsylvania textile mill for 20 cents a day and faithfully practicing his penmanship and arithmetic in his spare time in hopes of bettering himself.[15]

Workers' groups, at this time, were by no means united in their goals, but they were all for public schools that would teach reading, writing and arithmetic to every child. Seth Luther, a prototype of many later labor agitators, was a tall, lanky, tobacco-chewing Yankee who toured factory towns calling upon workers to condemn the by now deepening industrial poverty and worsening conditions of child labor. He was an outspoken advocate of public schools and adult self-education. One of his crusades was for manual labor schools where, among other things, both rich and poor would learn the dignity of work.

Despite rhetoric and grand utopian designs, as well as genuine reforms, the need for educated industrial workers continued unmet. The manual training school concept was put forward as an answer. And the year of the American Centennial, 1876, was in many ways a watershed year for industrial education according to Lawrence A. Cremin. The Centennial Exhibition in Philadelphia attracted exhibitions from around the world and one of them became an inspiration. "It is said," Dr. Cremin writes, "that President John D. Runkle of the Massachusetts Institute of Technology was strolling through Machinery Hall one day when he happened upon the Russian display cases. American education was never the same thereafter."[16] Runkle had found the industrial education method developed by Victor Della Vos, director of the Moscow Imperial Technical School. Della Vos had organized his school with shops for instructing boys in a definite method for each trade skill. He analyzed trades according to their component skills and devised a pedagogical order combining drawings, models, and tools into a graduated series of supervised exercises by which students could become proficient in a trade. This method replaced the old construction shop training that failed to give students a true proficiency. That same year, MIT established instruction shops for engineering students and a new School of Mechanical Arts to offer *manual* education for *industrial* careers along with the scientific education curriculum.

President Runkle went on to develop and promote a general theory of education based on manual training. He argued that the old apprenticeship system had correctly combined intellectual and manual arts. This educational ideal had been destroyed by the rise of an industrial system too committed to specialization in manufacture and by a public school system too focused on mental training. Manual education, however, offered restoration of a balanced education combining mental and manual skills. Most importantly, Runkle argued, it would realistically prepare students for enlightened and productive life in modern industrial society.

Calvin M. Woodward of Washington University in St. Louis joined the manual training supporters: a three-year secondary program carefully balancing intellectual and manual education was established at the university in 1879. Woodward argued that traditional education had excluded

32

the manual arts "because they were suspected of being useful"—a policy unfair, unproductive, and shortsighted. The "productive, toiling classes" had equal right to personal enrichment and increased productivity through education, he said, and he was quick to point out that manual training had a fringe benefit. Labor problems associated with uneducated, unintelligent workers would disappear.[17]

Manual training schools were established, accepted, attended and supported, but not for the high ideals of their proponents. Manual education students sought a route to better occupations and more remunerative employment. Apprenticeships by this time were severely limited by labor unions in an effort to control entry into the trades; to union distress vocational education offered another way around their control of the labor market. Corporate management, on the other hand, supported manual training schools because they freed business from the expense and responsibility for some training and freed them from union apprentice restrictions. The manual training schools plodded toward turning students into workers while industrialization galloped toward ever-newer technology.

Meanwhile, on a more advanced level of education, the federal government saw fit to act. For combined reasons of industrial, military and agricultural education needed for the expanding America—and with a little political bargaining thrown in—Congress passed the Morrill Land Grant Act in 1862. States that established colleges to train students in scientific farming, engineering and military science would be granted huge tracts of federal land under its terms to provide financial support for the program designed to increase technical knowledge and leadership to keep progress rolling toward unlimited prosperity. As a result of the Morrill Act more than 70 state colleges and universities were established.

EDUCATION FOR PRODUCTIVITY AND ENRICHMENT

Still, educational efforts could not provide for industrial change. Skilled mechanics in American industry were not being replaced so much by cheaper, unskilled immigrant labor in the latter nineteenth and early twentieth centuries as they were by cheaper, *skilled machines*. There was now unprecedented opportunity for those with an education to move into supervisory or white-collar positions with the unskilled, uneducated masses moving into the position of tending the skilled technology. This constant flux in the occupational distribution of industrial wage earners caused by the new machinery required *reeducation* of workers that would keep the labor force as finely tuned and up-to-date as the machinery. Only individual industries could offer—or afford—this type of situation-specific instruction.

Development of in-house educational systems was basically education for productivity. Education, whether of the "whole environment" sort offered by the textile manufacturers of the 1830s or the technical training refined later in the century, represented an investment by business. Making this investment required a fundamental concept on management's part: the worker is a form of capital. Corporate leaders expressed their policies toward education and training in a variety of patterns.

In a letter to Charles H. Bigelow, engineer of the Merrimack River dam and president of the new Franklin Library Association in Lawrence, Massachusetts, the great mill owner Abbott Lawrence offered both a $1,000 grant and this policy:

> There will soon gather round a large number of mechanics and others who will desire to obtain a knowledge of the higher mechanical arts. You will probably receive into your large mechanical shop . . . a number of apprentices, who are to be trained to the use of tools. The more thorough the education you give them, the more skillfully the tools will be used when placed in their hands. . . . I feel a deep interest in this question of educating men, who can take care of themselves, and do something to develop the mental resources of the present and future generations, as well as to make constructions [sic] to the common stock of practical knowledge and national resources of this great union.[18]

Cheney Brothers Silk Mills in Manchester, Connecticut—the nation's largest silk producer in the 1880s—provides an instance of broad company commitment to employee education and welfare. In addition to extensive

34

tract housing for workers, they built a large hall for workers' lectures, concerts and political meetings. They built schools. Their labor policies attracted national attention for many years first because of the firm's benevolent paternalism and then because they introduced "scientific management" and employed pioneer industrial psychologist Walter Dill Scott to formulate aptitude and performance ratings for workers.[19]

During this period of intense public and private sector interest in education for youth and workers came wide interest in the education of preschoolers, in part to lay the foundation for future industrial workers. The first kindergarten was established in St. Louis in 1873. By the turn of the century, there were about 3,000 kindergartens in America and the movement, devoted to preparing tiny citizens for their roles as healthy, productive adults, quickly spread.

Educational institutions of every sort—public, private, elementary, secondary, junior college, land grant schools, adult and juvenile vocational schools—were concerned with developing programs that would meet industry's need for workers. This national obsession with industrial progress moved historian Charles A. Beard to extravagance and in 1915 he wrote:

> More attention than ever is now being given to the problem of how education may best fit the pupils for their tasks as bread winners and as citizens. No subject calculated to throw light upon the problems of the world's work is being neglected. In university laboratories experiments are being conducted along all lines which may improve the quality and enlarge the quantity of wealth produced. . . . American democracy is trying the great experiment of combining learning with what the Greeks regarded as the "vulgar" pursuit of earning a living.[20]

Such exuberance was justifiable. By 1910, according to the National Society for the Promotion of Industrial Education, 29 states had provided some form of industrial education. Of these school systems, ten had technical high schools, 18 offered manual training and 11 included industrial and trade courses in their public education requirements; 25 of these states had enacted such legal requirements within the past decade.[21]

In that same year, a polygamous marriage of convenience took place when educators, labor, agriculture, and industry joined to lobby for federal support of a uniform program of straight trade education in the public schools. Until then public education advocates, agriculturalists, and industrial interests had engaged in parallel movements trying to mobilize resources for scientific and vocational education. The nationwide campaign for a federal vocational education bill was a tumultuous one, especially between the opposing American Federation of Labor and the supporting National Association of Manufacturers, but it was a successful one.

The Federal Commission on National Aid to Vocational Education was appointed in 1914 and in an exemplary business-like manner, submitted its report on time and spent only two-thirds of its funds. It strongly advocated vocational education. World War I made industrial education a national priority. In 1917 Congress passed the Smith-Hughes Act granting federal support to public vocational education in industrial arts, agricultural and domestic sciences.

Again, the complaints heard in the nineteenth century about manual training schools were raised. Industrial education instructors were isolated from innovation, machinery was obsolete by the time it reached classrooms. Within a decade Julius Klein observed:

> In order to keep pace with the stream of economic changes that are engulfing one trade after another, business has in self-defense been compelled to resort to much more aggressive educational campaigns for the building up of trained personnel. . . . The number of pupils in American vocational schools has risen from 265,000 in 1920 to more than 752,000 in 1925. Industry has taken upon itself not only the endowment of such establishments, but also the advancement of educational efforts within its own ranks.[22]

CORPORATION SCHOOLS

One response to developing human resources for industry's needs was the individual corporation school, the predecessor of the modern corporate classroom. These schools, which began at least as early as 1872, had no uniform structure; flexibility enhanced their utility for industry. Some corporations devised full-time classroom programs, others used a work-

36

study approach, and some permitted study at outside educational institutions. Classes were offered in both basic "cultural education" and training for upper-level occupations. Corporations found themselves educational providers of everything from English for non-English-speaking workers to courses in specialized products and methods, technical courses, advertising, salesmanship, business accounting, and management theory.[23]

Dr. Charles Steinmetz of General Electric, an early promoter of corporation schools, described them in 1914:

> A corporation school . . . is an elementary school conducted by
> a corporation to Americanize alien railway labor, for instance;
> or a commercial school with university class rooms, and some-
> times university lectures and credit; or a technical school with
> a course extending, as in one corporation, through four years
> of work of company worktime, demanding two hours each day,
> and a total of 10,960 hours in all, for bonus and a diploma.[24]

In 1913 some 35 prominent corporations sent top officials to organize together the National Association of Corporation Schools, which was to provide a forum to exchange ideas and information on employee training and to collect data on "successful and unsuccessful" programs. The ranks grew to 200 corporations, including many of the big names of today: Aetna Life Insurance, McGraw-Hill, E.I. duPont De Nemours, and so on. Not only do lists indicate a truly national body with corporations from Denver, Cincinnati, Minneapolis and other places, but membership became international, reaching 16 foreign countries. British companies set up their own Association for the Advancement of Education in Industry, patterned after the NACS.[25]

One company was a prime mover—the New York Edison Company. Thinking about developing educational work for employees, it sent F.C. Henderschott on the road to consult with other industrial executives across the country. From this journey came the Association, which New York Edison continued to support financially throughout its existence. National Cash Register, also in the initial group, contributed money and services, and described its training programs, along with General Electric's representative, on the first convention's platform.

Although the staff always had difficulty in collecting uniform data on individual company programs (as is the case today), they reported that 60,000 students were attending classes in 1916. Were these corporation schools educationally sound? One appraisal, comparing the corporation schools with the regular public schools of the period, found the former superior in responsiveness to students, recitation technique, and mental discipline; the latter were superior in teaching, breadth of vision, and promotion of general cultural education.[26]

One motif recurs in nearly every statement of objectives for the Association: to create reciprocal relations with established educational institutions and influence them to offer courses "to meet more fully the needs of industry and commerce . . . and to encourage all branches of literature, science, and art, or any of them, that pertain to industry and commerce." The motif, with a few exceptions, became a mere echo with little answer from established institutions. New York University gave a couple of courses to train corporation teachers and directors of company education, as did the Carnegie Institute of Technology. Individual professors from those institutions and Dartmouth, the Wharton School, and Tufts were active in Association affairs from time to time, and Dr. Lee Galloway of NYU joined as an early organizer of the Association, but professional participation did not basically or generally change institutional curricula. Widespread development of schools of business on university campuses came later.

Two exceptions, admired by the Association, were the Universities of Pittsburgh and Cincinnati, which had work-study programs for technical training. Cincinnati's was especially notable and graduated large numbers of engineers from its five-year program combining on-the-job training with study.

On the whole, however, corporations continued to provide their own training for employees, and they wanted no outside controls. At one point, when considering incorporation in the State of New York, the Association found it required the permission of the Board of Regents "which would then control the corporation schools in that state, while similar schools in other states would be controlled by the corresponding Departments of Education." They later incorporated in Delaware.

38

The first draft of objectives of the Association carried a theme that was dropped initially but resurfaced repeatedly in more diplomatic words. At first the idea was to see which programs were most effective so that "further and useless expenditure" on the unsuccessful programs could be eliminated. Later, the word "efficiency" took over—efficiency of the individual employee and efficiency in the industry.

From the restated purposes and many committee reports, attitudinal and organizational changes occurring in business became historically apparent. Reports from the period of World War I show the NACS joining the national effort and offering aid to President Woodrow Wilson "in investigating the industrial training of children, in the reeducating of crippled soldiers, and in cooperation with the Council on National Defense for Industrial Training for the War Emergency."[27]

Corporation Continuation Schools appeared, psychological testing of trade skills and abilities entered; training for foreign commerce, unskilled labor and Americanization courses were started. Beyond corporation schoolrooms, activities of the Association embraced human relations problems, profit and stock sharing plans, benefits in general, company restaurants, rest rooms, athletic activities, and "all other activities commonly known as welfare plans." Such remarks are reminiscent of earlier "company town" schemes like that of the Cheney Brothers, but less paternalistic, and educational training formed a larger part of the corporate program.

MANAGEMENT TRAINING AND PERSONNEL

"Executive Training" first appeared as a report at the convention in 1919 and became an absorbing concern. Since the executive was management and responsible for education of workers, the wider term "personnel relationships" gained attention. The Association's name shifted from "Schools" to "Training" in order to broaden the concept of its functions.

Meanwhile, a parallel organization had developed, the National Association of Employment Managers, later called the Industrial Relations Association of America. In contrast to the NACS, it started as a local effort and, largely because of the World War, was catapulted into a national organization. It had closer ties to Chambers of Commerce and the United States Department of Labor. In fact, on the occasion of voting for a national body, one delegate heatedly inquired who had "the right to direct any gigantic movement of this kind" and wanted it "recommended by someone close to the Secretary of Labor."

A lone woman, Mrs. Jane C. Williams of the Plimpton Press in Norwood, Massachusetts, was on the first executive committee of the national organization, and the convention in that year, 1918, voted to recommend to its local chapters that they should "take in women on the same basis as men." And the subject was not dropped. At the Chicago Convention in 1920, attended by 2,500 delegates, one section meeting was titled *Women* and a major address concerned the status of women in industry.

Almost half of the topics on that Chicago agenda were similiar to those on the NACS program 12 days later in New York City. Membership of the two organizations overlapped as well. Thus it came about that the two groups merged in 1922, calling themselves the National Personnel Association, and in the following year it became the American Management Association, well known today. Management was the overriding interest; education and training were its responsibility.

Education for industrial leadership was taking on new directions and greater sophistication. The Wharton School had been founded in 1881 and schools of business at the University of Chicago (1894), the University of California (1898) and Harvard (1908). After World War I, many colleges and universities responded to industrial need for managerial level personnel with business education programs.

Management, as a concept of professional activity using a body of knowledge that could be organized and taught, was a modern occupational distinction. Before the war, Frederick Winslow Taylor developed a theory that called for "a complete mental revolution on the part of the working man" and every other level of business activity. The "complete mental revolution" would be the application of Taylor's "scientific management" theories—the engineering of human productivity with the highest degree of efficiency.[28]

The human relations theory of management gained new ground in the 1920s and interrupted the popularity of "scientific management." This impetus for the human relations approach came about when a group from the Harvard Business School studied managerial-worker experiments being conducted at the Western Electric Company plant in Cicero, Illinois. The researchers concluded that the engineering approach was utterly inadequate for dealing with people. The project also established that within a large organization there were small, informal, but highly effective networks used by employees to disseminate information and get the work done. The application of social and behavioral sciences began in management education.[29] As these theories have evolved, the idea of the employee as a whole human resource has again come forward, as it did in the textile mills of the 1830s. Investment in the education and well-being of this resource has evolved as both goal and justification in the developing modern corporate philosophy of education.

Chester I. Barnard of the Bell System was an early and bold advocate of the well-rounded executive as a wise corporate investment. Himself a man of extraordinary intellectual accomplishments, Barnard had a deep interest in exploring methods of developing management resources for the future. As vice-president of operations for the Bell Telephone Company of Pennsylvania from 1922 to 1927 he was able to act on some of his innovative ideas. He arranged with the University of Pennsylvania for special courses in the humanities for his promising younger executives—a program that was to be revived and expanded by one of these young men 30 years later.

As the Great Depression ended and industry geared up to fight World War II, industry found its work force depleted by the Armed Services. Corporations found once again that they either had to train their workers or depend upon public education to do so. Since the early days of the Industrial Revolution, self-reliance had proved the better course. After World War II, with intense utilization of new technologies refined during the war and faced with heavy consumer demand, large-scale corporate education programs were undertaken.

Some corporate courses grew directly from war production experience. One example is Northrop's program to train for the aircraft industry that later developed into a full-blown university. Others, like General Motors

Institute that had started in the 1920s, expanded dramatically and added the latest fields of study.

The 1950s saw colossal growth in corporate education and training for foremen and supervisors, factory operators, technical and professional personnel, junior and senior executives and, to a lesser extent, clerical staff. Many new alignments and contracts were made with colleges and universities to buy faculty expertise, particularly for management needs and technical engineering courses. Western Electric, IBM, AT&T, International Harvester and General Electric were among the leaders in educational efforts for their personnel, and programs were growing to sizeable dimensions. GE, for example, was offering 1,500 separate courses in 1956, enrolling 32,000 employees at an annual expenditure of $35 to $40 million.

IBM was turning laboratory technicians who had a two-year technical diploma or equivalent military or industrial experience into assistant engineers by giving them a regular 12-week course, 40 hours a week, with classroom demonstration and laboratory work, using standard texts as well as specially prepared materials. It was not unusual for company classrooms to use college texts midst the wide array of courses being given.

Two studies done in the late 1950s and early 1960s describe the scene in larger corporations and show the pattern of the modern classroom of the 1980s which clearly began at least three decades ago.[30] Both used questionnaires on fairly large samples, received good returns and followed up with interviews. Clark and Sloan had a 72 percent return on 482 firms and Oscar Serbein of Stanford's Graduate School of Business had 276 useful replies on a sample of 300 large companies.

Both surveys had the familiar troubles of getting at costs of company programs, but agreed that the larger ones were spending more on education than some large educational institutions. Clark and Sloan claimed that expenditures per student not infrequently were two and one-half to three times the national average for conventional classrooms in four-year colleges.[31] And they recognized "that a new sector is being added to the traditional pattern of American public and private education."

Categories of subject matter being taught formally and informally are similar to today's pattern of training with orientation programs for the individual company most common. Next comes managerial development, human relations courses, technical and professional in fourth rank and general education courses last.[32] A broad definition for the last category included elementary and high school subjects like American history and government and avocational interests like ceramics, gardening, dancing, and painting.

Human relations courses reflect a fascination with role playing. Elton Mayo ran extensive experiments at the Hawthorne Works of Western Electric Company for 12 years ending in 1939, and his influence was pervasive for years. Another fashion of the fifties was Creative Thinking courses; nine of the ten largest corporations in the country offered them in one form or another. They saw results in the discovery of patentable ideas and new processes. In 1955 General Motors graduated 500 students from this sort of instruction and the Gary Plant of U.S. Steel had 1,400 graduates the following year.

In many ultramodern classrooms with the latest equipment, millions of adults were training for new processes, product diversification, multiplant development and decentralized organization in the large companies. Integrated programs—more than a course—were designed for maintaining flexible organizations and keeping abreast of the times. Belief in education was growing as a way of corporate life, and it grew into a continuous life process.

More than ever before, industry embraced the fact that the more educated person can be reeducated more efficiently. Corporations sought employees, particularly in the upper management level, who could move within the company and around the country. The edge has been called by John Kenneth Galbraith "the added mobility between occupations and regions that goes with education."[33]

Two case studies demonstrate how these broadly conceived notions of the educated employee were pursued and applied. In 1952 the Bell System returned to the University of Pennsylvania and the pioneering project of Chester Barnard. A new university-level humanities education program was undertaken for management employees in the belief that "the study of the humanities is of more long-range value than study of the day-to-day problems of the manager."[34] Creation of the Institute of Humanistic

Studies at the University of Pennsylvania was an eclectic departure in corporate management education and included courses in the humanities, physical and social sciences, philosophy, art, music and drama. A yearly average of 20 hand-picked young middle management men attended the ten-month program between 1953 and 1960. Ingenuity and flexibility were high among the criteria for selection.

Another upper-level education program was conceived by Bell in collaboration with Dartmouth and Williams Colleges in 1955. An eight-week program was designed to help train "a better manager and a more valuable member of his community." The program, developed by college faculty, had three broad objectives:[35]

1. to broaden interests and extend the habit of inquiry and reflection;
2. to sharpen awareness of the current social, political, and economic climate and the conferee's place in it;
3. to lay the groundwork for a substantial program of self development.

Swarthmore College, Northwestern University and Carleton College offered similar broad-based management courses for Bell. Some programs lasted until 1970, but they became controversial and a source of tension. Attending executives worried that evaluation of their performance might adversely affect their career within the company, even though the goal was to enhance and guide executive development rather than create a climate of competition.

During this same period, IBM developed its extensive, high-quality education program. IBM worked primarily in house to educate its own personnel, including its sales staff, and customers' personnel. After about a decade of broad corporate educational development, each of the divisions of IBM had an educational function. Extensive course work was given in: sales and customer training, customer engineering (service), engineering, manufacturing, programming, management development, and voluntary and extension education after-hours. IBM had already established its well-defined and famous human resources policy and its corporate culture concept. Graduate programs were offered in house for IBM engineers, including Ph.D. fellowships and masters' scholarships that brought in

44

Syracuse University graduate faculty as in-house instructors. Career-long education had become established at IBM.

Training in all its varieties was entering more and more companies. Corporations had recognized the importance of employee education virtually from the birth of the Industrial Revolution. Industrial leaders consistently supported public education and particularly programs to train more competent workers. Their philosophy generally reflected the words of Everitt Dean Martin when he wrote in 1928: "It is not so much as a guarantor of liberty as [it is] an agency of progress—prosperity—that democracy and industry support the school."[36] It was true in the days of Horace Mann when the public school system started, true when the federally funded land grant schools and vocational schools were founded, it continues to be true as corporations seek to collaborate with universities and colleges.

In the long history of interrelationship between industry and the educational system, each has contributed to the growth of the other. Just as industry and economic development fostered the establishment of schools, U.S. education has, in turn, provided workers, expertise, and leadership for industry. But the education and training programs of industry and the traditional educational system have basically been parallel developments—not an integrated relationship. They certainly have never been synchronized, and traditional education has lagged behind industrial needs from the very beginning. No linkage between the two has ever been effective on any large scale.

Therefore, industry has steadily manned its own training centers and taken responsibility for the efficiency and educational growth of its workers. While in the nineteenth century industry was, for a time, taking the role of patron in training, today private industry is taking the role of mentor and educator.

CHAPTER III

Corporate Education: Structure and Methods

WRITING 25 YEARS AGO, Jay W. Forrester of the Sloan School of Management at MIT argued that, "some 25 percent of the total working time of all persons in the corporations should be devoted to preparation for their future roles. . . . The educational program must become an integral part of corporate life, not just a few weeks or months once in a lifetime at another institution."[1] Dr. Forrester's insight is reflected in the thinking and intent of leading companies today.

The role of business as educational provider has taken on new directions and deeper dimensions. There has been a dramatic increase in both the usual education programs and in imaginative learning environments for new technology, new products, and new marketplaces. The reason for industry's corporate education has remained unchanged since the days of Abbott Lawrence. The reason is the always changing nature of technology and its application in industry, the reason is the need of the corporation for the best possible worker. Productivity and enrichment of the worker, hence the company, are the goals.

The classrooms today are far from Lowell or the Mechanics Institute libraries. They surpass many universities in their sophistication both in the range of offerings and in the delivery systems and methods as well. They are not factory-bound, they are global, and a single corporation may be educating in New York, Rio de Janeiro, Tokyo, and Rome.

FACILITIES

Many large corporations have their own learning centers dedicated exclusively to the continuing education of their workers. It is estimated that

47

about 400 business sites presently include a building or a campus labeled "college, university, institute, or education center."[2]

Examples abound: Holiday Inn University, Dana University with its 3,000 students; NCR's Management College and its Computer Science Institute; Sun Institute with its Learning Center near corporate head-quarters in Radnor, Pennsylvania; ARCO's campus at Santa Barbara for top executives; New England Telephone's Learning Center at Marlboro, Massachusetts, that accommodates some 9,000 employees attending classes during the summertime; and Xerox's Learning Center in Leesburg, Virginia, probably the largest of them all.

Corporate campuses may look like traditional colleges with classrooms, computerized libraries, laboratories, gymnasiums, residence halls and din-ing rooms, but the corporate learning centers are more modern, sleek and up-to-date. Few display ivy-covered walls, but landscaping and good cam-pus maintenance means gardeners are around and money is spent. Res-idence facilities are often elegant and comfortable, designed for executives and managers. Lecture halls and classrooms have built-in visual aids and the latest communications technology.

The ambience here is very different from the collegiate setting; there is no leisurely chatting and loitering about campus. Behavior is purposeful, the atmosphere intense and concentrated, the age level older. Courses usually are short-term, schedules tight, goals explicit. Much of the content is clearly company-oriented regardless of the conceptual framework that embraces management theories. Considerable "homework" is expected each evening for class discussion the next day.

This is not to suggest, however, a staid formality either among the employee-students or with their teachers. Corporate classrooms have, in fact, a pronounced informality; first names are used immediately, and no special markers denote the president's or any other officer's parking places. In attitude, management is more horizontal—among equals—and less the vertical hierarchy associated with older industrial establishments.

Western Electric's Corporate Education Center in Princeton describes its 300-acre campus with justifiable pride: spacious private rooms with baths, an excellent cuisine, lighted tennis courts for a night game, and deer wandering about the landscape. Idyllic, but very serious business

48

too; the Center houses most of Western Electric's major management and engineering programs. Its equipment and communications facilities, of course, are technologically advanced and support effective, intensive courses.

IBM has several campuses in the United States and overseas. The company now is creating another at Thornwood, New York, to be opened in 1985. The new center will house IBM's oldest and best known in-house school, the Systems Research Institute, as well as the Manufacturing Technology Institute, the Quality Institute, and the Software Engineering Institute. Extensive designing and imaginative projections for IBM's educational needs have gone into planning what should be more than "state-of-the-art" educational facilities.

The larger corporate campuses with residence accommodations usually have athletic facilities and emphasize physical fitness, just as many of their courses emphasize personal stress management. As an IBM brochure puts it: "Management does not live by books alone;" hence, the fifth building of the complex on the IBM Armonk, New York, campus is a gymnasium for volleyball, basketball, exercise equipment, and so on. Besides outdoor tennis courts, each residence hall has table tennis and pool tables. (Oddly enough, despite almost unlimited facilities, no corporate campus seems to advertise a swimming pool, which should be most effective for middle-aged executives coping with stress!) Some 5,000 IBM'ers graduate each year from the Armonk campus where management training is highly structured. Managers are regularly required to study for set periods of time at each pivotal point as they progress in supervisory responsibility.

EDUCATIONAL STRUCTURE

Although many big companies use central facilities for special programs, the typical educational pattern within a corporation is much more diffuse. Instruction extends throughout operations and beyond company walls. Typically, a corporation buys some courses from vendors or middlemen, contracts with colleges or universities for special purposes, employs a college professor occasionally to teach an in-house course, joins consortia

49

for effective delivery systems for advanced technological programs, or pays tuition at schools for some employees to study individually. Most frequently, however, the corporation operates its own in-house system using its own corporate trainers. Companies prefer their own program; they can directly control it and adjust for changing purposes and content and introduce quickly new time frames and schedules.

Options are kept open on where and how courses are to be given within the company. It's called "distributive" education and it reaches throughout the company's units in this country and, for multinationals, the world. The pattern is toward decentralization and the ultimate goal is reaching the individual or group at the actual workplace.

At IBM, for example, each division handles its own education and is responsible for its curricular materials. The overall goal, however, is to create a worldwide educational system for its 103,000 technology professionals. The system will track an individual's record to see where more work is needed. Another IBM option for training technical personnel is a graduate work-study plan that had 2,600 participants in 1982. After one-half of the credits for the M.S. degree are completed on a part-time study basis, the person goes on to study full-time; Ph.D. candidates are all studying on a full-time basis. These programs are conducted at universities, not in house. For the worldwide Field Training System, computer-aided instruction is used along with other methods, and training takes place both in branch offices and central facilities. Opportunities for up-to-date technological competency and improvement are innumerable.

Texas Instruments' educational networks encompass the entire organization. The complex system includes internal training at TI, educational assistance (tuition refund) for outside courses, and commercial seminar participation. Through a computerized Training and Education Management System, corporation headquarters can retrieve information on every course, the number enrolled both currently and accumulative, evaluations of the course and instructor, costs and where they are charged. Any employee's training record (password protected) is available with all courses taken, when, and where. Pertinent facts to manage the company's total educational functions are at hand, and the system supports training information needs right down to group levels.

50

Worldwide networks of TI Learning Centers, as well as regional activities oriented for product buyers, are registered in the massive and impressive system. Data assembled from all segments of TI's education and training, programmed in the master computer, yield answers to a multitude of questions that are vital in decision making: toll-taking for preparedness of personnel to undertake new tasks, cost factors, and strategies for future directions.

Smaller companies, if they have training at all, offer fewer options. They are more apt to make cooperative arrangements with outside institutions and vendors when necessary and possible. The appearance, however, of educational delivery systems like the National Technological University could widen options for small firms that need advanced technical training, and there are increasing numbers of small firms such as those engaged in high-tech and related fields. The company needs only to agree to cooperate for five years in order to permit enrolled employees to complete NTU courses. No direct financial underwriting is required by NTU, but most companies pay tuition costs for their employees.

Communications and media advances will undoubtedly multiply options—now open only to the giants—for smaller companies. Packaged self-study materials, videotaped courses, and computer managed or assisted instruction of many types already provide extensive learning opportunities at the workplace and at home.

TRAINING'S POSITION IN THE COMPANY

A most important factor determining the extent and success of an industry's training program is the position of the person responsible for it. The higher the officer in charge of education, the more it reflects the commitment of the corporation to the program. To succeed, the chief executive officer has to want it. And the appointment of a corporate level executive for education will have the greatest impact on managers down the line, who permit the employee time off for study. It's their budgets that contribute a healthy part of the education cost. Thus, there can be a lot of top-level talk to encourage training, but for it to really happen depends on decisions down the line. To counter possible resistance, the

51

president and other corporate officers will appear in corporate classrooms to talk about company policies and procedures. The presence of top executives obviously underscores the importance of the training session.

Similarly, the position of trainers, as corporate classroom teachers are called, is vital to the effectiveness of education in the company. If too many are part-time, or if they are rotated too frequently, the program will lack cohesion and continuity. If the trainer's job is seen as a dead end—without promotional opportunities and possible advancement—the best talent will not want to become trainers. Corporate classrooms have problems not unlike the traditional educational system in terms of the teacher's position and the reward system.

Trainers have their own professional associations such as the American Society for Training and Development that has 50,000 members. The society has its well-known *Training and Development Journal*; another professional periodical is *Training, The Magazine of Human Resources Development*, that provides an annual survey of employee training and development activities, and reports regularly on subjects of concern. The October 1984 issue, for example, indicates that trainers are getting more budget control, more decision-making authority, and more respect. So signs are optimistic for the trainer's role.

And it should be noted that trainers' ranks are growing. Estimates from *Training* indicate that there are some 250,000 full time trainers and another 500,000 teaching part time in American organizations both public and private. They constitute a large work force themselves.

METHODS IN CORPORATE CLASSROOMS

Teaching methods in the corporate classroom are often less revolutionary, less experimental and avant garde than might be expected in facilities equipped more often than not with the latest audiovisual materials and computers. In fact, many still use the lecture method and discussion, or the familiar seminar for small groups. In this respect, corporate classrooms resemble traditional colleges, but not all companies are satisfied with the stand-up teacher or the sit-down talking instructor. Methods are tried, adjusted and changed, so one finds a much broader range of teaching-learning techniques here than in conventional education.

Dana University, when developing teaching strategies for particular courses, decided that since "most conferees are people who work on their feet and are on the go all day, rather than 'desk people,' " emphasis should be on variety in student activities with very little lecture. Consequently, techniques include role playing, team projects, case studies and other group activities rather than "sit-down" sessions.[3]

IBM's Manufacturing Technology Institute is changing required lectures for beginning students to packaged courses taken individually as a prerequisite for admission. This shift in teaching procedure will save time and money; it will guarantee a shared body of basic knowledge among students. In contrast, IBM's training for sales service and customers has shifted back to more classroom work, away from the programmed instruction that was judged not particularly successful.[4] Adjustments go in both directions.

Above all there are moves to increase instructional effectiveness, and several methods may be combined for certain purposes. While some corporate trainers see deficiences in computer-assisted or managed instruction, it nevertheless is used extensively, just as films, programmed materials, and individual self-studies are used for particular purposes. Computer networks that link voice, graphics, text, motion, and audio are coming into their own as miniature and completely personalized "classrooms." The assortment of teaching methods employed is exceedingly wide and experimental, especially when compared to the average college or university classroom.

Instructional *efficiency* characterizes corporate training, but it is not obtrusive in a learning atmosphere that offers variety and flexibility. The corporate calendar differs markedly from the collegiate lock-step of two semesters and four years. Business-based courses are given practically any time and for any necessary length of time from a few hours, a day, or perhaps 48-hour weeks, semesters, or a year. Time is determined by purpose.

Polaroid's Technical and Business Writing course meets for 20 two-hour sessions on company time, Mondays and Wednesdays from 2:30 to

4:30 p.m. from September 14 to December 2. The time allows for skills practice. Another Polaroid course, Time Management, lasts just one day. Not all companies appear to be as generous as Polaroid in allowing work hours for course taking; some schedule early mornings or late afternoons, overlapping slightly with company time. Others, however, give employees full time off for two weeks, and much longer for outside advanced degree work. Patterns are extremely diverse, but overall, courses tend toward the shorter time frames, especially compared to conventional colleges, and they are content-intensive.

Convenience is a determining factor in deciding where the course is given, whether it is part-time, what time of day it is offered, and if it is packaged for use in the home setting. All of these flexible features put the company—if it is so inclined—into the larger education industry now developing course materials for sale to consumers at large.

Teaching in the corporate classroom is by objective, like management by objective: a planned and stated goal, controls, and measurement of performance. Course development, especially in large firms with central education offices, follows careful procedures, starting with assessment of need for the instruction. Given that, close collaboration then follows with operational personnel who know what they want and help determine clear objectives. Sometimes there is a design committee of experts on the subject, or a steering group that oversees course development. A pilot course is tried and criticized, often by employee-students as well as by topic experts and curricular specialists. Questions are: Will students be able to meet objectives? Is content technically correct? After a ''fine tuning'' the course goes into the company's published course list. That process follows Dana University's pattern, but it also generally describes course development at the Sun Institute, Hewlett-Packard, NCR, and many others.

Possible overemphasis on in-house training raises potential problems for a company's education system. Since corporate trainers usually come from inside and employees are the students, corporate policies and attitudinal loyalties are all-pervasive. The corporate ''culture'' envelops the classroom and programs can become in-bred—incestuous—raising ques-

54

tions about freedom of inquiry and opinion, particularly when questions differ from the established ethos. These are very real hazards that need to be guarded against with awareness and judicious use of options and outside contacts.

Trainers, selected for company experience along with their subject matter expertise, increasingly have their own teacher training courses and practice teaching sessions. Hewlett-Packard, for example, gives a workshop on Learning and Teaching Techniques with textbooks on *Principles of Adult Learning* and *Learner-Centered Training*. Teacher performance is evaluated and student achievement assessed according to objectives.

Policies concerning grades or achievement records for employees differ among companies. Some feel grades inhibit class participation and open discussion and that there will be fear if performance records are reported to the boss. In these cases the employee record shows only the course taken. Other companies, in contrast, report achievement on the employee's permanent record just as grade averages are required for tuition refunds for outside courses. The justification here is that the record promotes motivation and performance. Another approach is to describe the employee-student "potential" and to record particular achievement areas.

RESEARCH IN THE LEARNING PROCESS

One of the most promising activities in some corporate education centers is research into how people learn. Inquiry into the learning process, cognitive as well as affective, is a growing concern not only for implementation within corporate classrooms but, especially, for improving effectiveness of courses being created for the public market. Commercial organizations in the software business are pouring large sums of money into investigating human learning patterns to make their products superior and more lasting in results.

New insights into the educational process are coming from corporate classrooms—not from colleges and universities. Higher education has done little to learn about teaching and learning. The university's instructional mode has scarcely changed over the past 50 years. Educational innovations are few and often of only marginal impact. F. Reif continues his analysis:

> Nor is this situation surprising, since the university, unlike any progressive industry, is not in the habit of improving its own performance by systematic investment in innovative research and development. Indeed, the resources allocated by the university to educational innovation are usually miniscule or non-existent. . . . Is it too farfetched to suggest that the university should take education at least as seriously as the Bell Telephone Company takes communication?[5]

Reif's charge is fair. Seldom has interest in the learning process, its difference among individuals, and the implications for classroom methods been expressed in educational halls, much less supported and rewarded.

Turning to corporate education centers, one finds interesting research projects and experiments being conducted by enthusiastic teams. Leeds and Northrup University (Development Institute) was born for just such research and to sustain developmental momentum. When told to design courses to fit L&N's needs—and admonished against presenting "dry lectures"—Bob Eddy and John Kellow proceeded to "undry" the learning process by considering learning models and instructional techniques, trying them out, and finally creating their own conceptual framework: a three-stage model for the learning process. Learning is defined as behavioral change for courses with that objective. The process model's stages are:

1. Conceptual Awareness. The student understands the concept involved.
2. Emotional Choice. The student emotionally buys into the concept and vows to employ it.
3. Behavioral Change. The concept, through repetition, is pressed into the student's behavior pattern until it becomes normal behavior.[6]

Leeds and Northrup's is basically subjective work as they point out. It is not a scientifically tested hypothesis, but rather "experiential gut feelings

56

resulting from several years of intense, exciting efforts to launch a corporate 'university' and decide upon its training models, philosophies, and techniques." Their "Return on Investment Curve" showing four degrees of student response and their techniques developed for maintaining and guiding group dynamics are most provocative and suggest effective methods.

Along different and more scientifically tested lines, David A. Kolb developed LSI (Learning-Style Inventory) for McBer and Company. It is an individualized learning analysis that the American Management Association has chosen as the diagnostic tool for its new degree program in managerial competency. In this inventory, students rank their own learning styles on a set of nine choices that transfer onto a four-pronged grid representing what Kolb identifies as the learning modes of concrete experience, active experimentation, reflective observation, and abstract conceptualization. This, in turn, suggests variations of experiential learning methods for the individual and forms the basis for designing the student's work and study program.

Digital Equipment's Corporate Manager for Educational Services, Del Lippert, speaks with conviction and detailed knowledge of their research on the ways people approach learning. Their analysis—more directly cognitive than Kolb's for experiential learning—leads to combinations of four approaches: concrete, abstract, sequential, and random.

Analysis of how the student learns is basic to the determination of teaching techniques embodied in Digital's IVIS (Interactive Video Information System) that integrates communication technologies providing text, voice, motion, graphics, and audio elements. The architecture—network—reflects the complexity of teaching; the goal is to "clone" the professor, giving ample options for individualized response to students who are revealing to the system their personal learning attitudes and skills: when they are bored and slow to answer, when their reply is quick and accurate. Thus far, Digital claims IVIS-trained students learn up to 53 percent faster and with better retention than students taught by conventional methods.

Digital has gone to market with IVIS and its testing ground grows; so does its continuing research into the learning process. Courses can be taught more effectively with increased interaction and combinations of methods, whether in the classroom or in the gaining abilities of artificial intelligence interacting with individuals anywhere. Challenging information comes from corporate research on how people learn, and the results are being tried out both within corporate classrooms and in shaping software for the public.

When the results of exploration into the learning process are combined with corporate leaders' insistence on efficiency and evaluation of training programs, industry's education will take another leap forward. Already its effectiveness merits our attention.

CHAPTER IV

The Curriculum and Quality

THE CURRICULUM of corporate classrooms has broadened markedly in recent years. Courses of study now seek to educate the whole person and to put the work of industry in a larger social, economic, and political context. Indeed, the corporate curriculum increasingly parallels the work of the nation's colleges and schools, ranging from the teaching of English and computation to post-doctoral study and research.

There are five major areas of corporate study—Basic Skills Instruction, Management and Executive Training, Technical and Scientific Study, Sales, Service and Customer Training, and General Education. In these areas, relationships of corporate courses to the educational establishment are considered along with the quality of corporate instruction.

BASIC SKILLS INSTRUCTION

Much public attention has centered on the academic deficiences of high school graduates. Nowhere are those deficiencies more immediately apparent than in the workplace. The problem becomes greater when one adds school dropouts, adults from minority backgrounds, and recent immigrants who may be illiterate in English. Businesses have been constrained to employ minorities as part of affirmative action legislation and their own sense of social justice. There are more and more black and Hispanic youth who must be helped to find jobs. Hence, even though many companies carefully screen applicants for employment and frequently give their own academic achievement tests, they nevertheless find it necessary to provide remedial work in the elementary skills of reading, writing and arithmetic.

A critical report on "Basic Skills in the U.S. Work Force," based on a survey of companies, labor unions, and school systems, was issued in 1983 by the Center for Public Resources.[1] The study defined basic academic capabilities broadly: in addition to the three R's, sciences at the high school level were considered essential as well as the skills of speaking, listening and reasoning or critical thinking. To ask a question clearly and coherently, to follow instructions, to draw a reasonable conclusion from information given—all were cited as examples of basic abilities needed.

Corporate respondees (184) were asked to rank the importance of various abilities necessary for different jobs. School systems' administrators (123) were asked simply to rank the same abilities for getting and holding a job as they perceived it. Comparison of the responses revealed most disturbing discrepancies between business and school executives:

> Mathematics, science, and speaking-listening skills represented the areas of greatest divergence, with corporate executives deeply concerned about low level skills and school officials evaluating students as adequately prepared to meet employment requirements.
>
> Moreover, business respondees expressed serious concern about the impact of those deficiencies not only on employability but also on the viability of retaining and promoting such employees to higher levels of responsibility within the corporation.[2]

In other words, the person who is deficient in basic abilities stands less chance of advancement in the company; the handicap may be for a lifetime in work. Furthermore, responses showed that school officials generally did not perceive mathematics and sciences as essential in preparing graduates for future employment.

The difference in perception between school and business leaders is not only discouraging: it explains why business must offer extensive high school-level courses at considerable cost, and why companies have increasingly sought cooperative arrangements with schools to produce graduates who are better equipped for the realities of the workplace.

Reading deficiencies did not appear to be as severe in the CPR study as they have in other reports, but 40 percent of corporations saw them as leading to serious problems. The operational impact of reading deficiencies was not just in hazardous situations where the worker could not read warning signs; most often, it was in loss of time and money when written instructions had to be given orally, for example, by lecturing on the use of computerized long-distance telephone dialing because employees could not read step-by-step instructions. An example of mere inconvenience was also given: one company that was receiving constant complaints about its cafeteria food finally discovered the cook could not read well enough to distinguish "tablespoon" from "teaspoon" in recipes.

Business leaders' concern about basic academic competence has been sharply heightened by changes in the nature of jobs. One executive explains that the "lift, place, take, put jobs" that could be performed regardless of worker education levels are rapidly being replaced by technology. Rote clerical jobs such as typing forms all day become extinct with the advent of the word processor. Technologies challenge more than industry, they challenge directly the schools' preparation of young people to live and work with them, they ask greater understanding of the processes and principles of their operation.

In the CPR study, 75 percent of the corporations carry out some type of basic skills programs within their company for employees. McGraw-Hill's "Numbers Skills Program" is reportedly used by many to teach accuracy in computation. A tachistoscope (a speedreading pacer adapted to work with numbers) is used along with filmstrips and trainee workbooks. Control Data's PLATO instructs individually in reading, math, and language arts. Materials developed by Lyman Steil with assistance from the Sperry Corporation are targeted at listening skills and used widely in industry. Many of these programs are easily adapted for school settings.

Many more courses—worthy of investigation by school systems—appear in corporate catalog listings in this study. High school equivalent courses or repeats include the following examples from several different types of companies:

MANUFACTURERS HANOVER
    Effective Communications - Listening
    Basic Arithmetic

Basic Speech - Grammar, Spelling, Punctuation
English as a Second Language I, II, III
Shorthand - Dictation and Dictaphone
Typing including Statistical Typing
Basic Writing Skills - Letter, Memo, Reports especially for technical professional personnel

POLAROID
High School Chemistry and Physics
Algebra and Trigonometry
Metric System
Literacy Training Tutorials
Reading Labs

NCR
Basic English Grammar
Effective Business Writing
Effective Technical Writing

IBM: SOFTWARE ENGINEERING INSTITUTE
Self-study courses in Algebra, Math Preparation and Review, Logical Expression

AMERICAN INSTITUTE OF BANKING — NEW YORK CITY
Reading and Study Skills Development
Reading and Writing English Skills for the Foreign Educated
Conversational English for the Foreign Educated
Speech

CHRYSLER CORPORATION
Reading Skills
Introduction to Writing
Writing Skills
Speech Skills
Accelerated Reading

CONSOLIDATED EDISON
Effective Reading
Effective Listening

STANDARD OIL OF CALIFORNIA
  Better Letter Writing
  Put it in Writing
  Technical Writing
  Practical English and the Command of Words
  Effective Communicating

The examples are drawn at random from company course lists and in no way indicate the coverage in any one company. The repetition in course titles shows how pervasive and similar the problems are. The listing says a lot about basic academic deficiencies in the U.S. work force. And such courses are not limited to entry-level employees. Some of the same titles will be found in courses designed for management and other personnel categories at differing levels.

MANAGEMENT AND EXECUTIVE TRAINING

The education of managers and executives is one of the largest areas in corporate curricula, and its content is similar among different types of companies. After all, "management is management" and certain functions pertain regardless of the end product or service.

Management training also offers the clearest course sequence; it is scheduled at regular transition points in individual career development. Training progresses in linear fashion from the first supervisory assignment to first-line manager, middle management, and on to corporate-level executives. Or, as one company puts it: from non-manager to manager, to manager of managers, to functional manager, to general manager. No other curricular area is laid out in so orderly and logical a sequence—except perhaps the orientation program that introduces all new employees to the particular corporation.

To indicate purpose and content—what is taught in management training—courses are considered by functions rather than levels at which they occur. Goals are frequently behavioral, and courses draw content from the behavioral sciences, economics, humanities, and business education. There is often stress on financial aspects, as one would expect. Functionally, management curricula divide into four general areas:

Managing Time is a constant theme throughout industry. Whether it is "Time Management" and "Delegating Work" at Manufacturers Hanover, or "Effective Delegation" at Polaroid, or "Work Simplification" courses at Texas Instruments, efficient and effective use of work hours is obviously most important at all companies.

Managing People competes with, and may well surpass, the function of managing operations if, indeed, the two can be separated. Tremendous time, money, and energy go into courses like:

Selection Interviewing
Performance Appraisal
Team Building
Effective Work Relationships
Motivating Employees
Effective Listening
Conducting Effective Meetings
Making Presentations
Effective Leadership
Managing Conflict
Effective Negotiations
Problem Solving Processes
Coping with Stress in Organizational Life
Managing a Diverse Work Force
    Part I: Differences in Age
    Part II: Cultural Differences
Creative Thinking
Writing Workshops
Self-Development

These course titles are not peculiar to any one industry. They come directly from a variety of corporate catalogs—Standard Oil of California, New England Telephone, Kimberly-Clark, Polaroid, Manufacturers Hanover, Texas Instruments, and others.

And, these courses that focus on human development raise serious issues for colleges and universities because their goals often are completely consistent with the missions of established schools. Aside from basic skills of expression that should be expected of any graduate, key questions must be faced. If corporate education must spend so much time on personal relationships and team action, have schools and colleges been so individually oriented that students have not learned to work with others? Has individual development reached such a point that graduates are not prepared for cooperative action and group leadership unless they have engaged in *extra-curricular* activities? Team projects are typical in laboratory sciences. Why aren't there more in the social sciences and humanities? Why aren't there more in high schools and colleges generally? Team projects in no way deny individual differences or impede personal growth; to the contrary, they provide opportunities for contributions from different abilities and knowledge. They prepare for the collaborative efforts so obviously needed in the workplace—and generally in life. The challenge posed by personal development in corporate education cannot be ignored.

Managing Money also claims high stakes in corporate training for management positions. From basic accounting principles, computerized information systems, financial reporting, budgeting, and cost control, managers are introduced to company-specific practices and policies. Decision making and problem solving using alternative solutions in case studies, simulation techniques, and role playing are taught also for behavioral goals—with financial outcomes clarified.

Managing Production and Operations receives great attention in managerial training—along with personnel management. Again, among diverse firms the course titles are common even though content may differ with types of production. A sample:

Management Fundamentals
Management by Objectives
Data Collection and Analysis
Quality Training
Creativity at Your Job
Introducing Change

Computer-related and Information Systems
Mini- and Micro-Computer Applications Overview
Managing the Application Development Process

When, however, top executive management programs are reviewed, a very different type of curriculum appears. Although courses continue to emphasize the particular corporate culture, strategic planning, and decision making, much broader concerns enter: outside environmental factors, public policy issues, governmental relations and international politics, ethics and corporate social responsibility. At the top levels, more outside experts enter the training seminar, or the seminar may move from the corporate center to a university campus or to a special institute. Executive programs frequently are of longer duration than other company training courses. University sessions often run for a month or two; peers from other companies in the United States and abroad participate along with experienced persons from government and other fields. The mix of participants and subjects is wide; the focus is broad and horizons are extended.

Bob Swiggett, the philosopher-founder and chairman of the board of Kollmorgen Corporation with 5,000 employees, leads his own Kolture Workshops 12 times a year to "keep the fires burning and spread them broadly."[3] His participants come well prepared with about 40-hours reading from McGregor's *The Human Side of Enterprise*; Alexis de Tocqueville's *Democracy in America*; Martin Luther King, Jr.'s "Letter from the Birmingham Jail;" Machiavelli's *The Prince*, and numerous articles on leadership, innovation and economics. At a three-day session, Swiggett, in Socratic fashion, examines the philosophical issues that inform the company's culture and asks, "Do you think this philosophy can work at Kollmorgen, and how can we improve it?"

Some programs are less company slanted and the context is broader, especially if they are run by universities or outside institutes. They are reminiscent of the Bell System's humanities programs in the 1950s and 1960s. The Aspen Institute for Humanistic Studies started in the early 1950s with the vision and leadership of Walter Paepcke, head of the Container Corporation of America. His idea was to give busy, often harried corporate officers an opportunity to join with colleagues from other companies for two weeks to discuss readings from the Great Books and ideas that are applicable to today's issues—and do so in a beautiful place like Aspen, Colorado. Moderators were not from the business world, and outside resource guests were invited both to spark and inform arguments.

Aspen's Executive Seminars still follow the original format but the readings—sent well in advance to participants—now extend to contemporary writers and thinkers. In addition to selections from Plato, Aristotle, the Bible, Machiavelli, Locke, Adam Smith, the U.S. Constitution, Marx, Dostoyevsky, Darwin, Freud, and Martin Luther King, Jr.'s ''Letter,'' readings may include Mao Zedong and others whose thinking is pertinent to the modern corporation and society, justice, freedom, and the building of a more humane world.

Over the years, more than 5,000 top-echelon managers have attended Aspen seminars; some 55 corporations currently support the program. On the list are many large, socially-minded firms such as Aetna Life, American Express, Corning Glass, Dayton-Hudson, General Foods, and General Mills. There are banks, brokerage firms, and pension funds; corporations from Sweden, West Germany, and Venezuela; and many oil companies such as ARCO, Gulf, Mobil, Exxon, and Sun are active supporters.

Spin-offs from the original Aspen format are shorter seminars on The Corporation in Contemporary Society and AT&T's special sessions for middle management that emphasize public policy concerns and exposure to society's problems, including a jail visit to interview both prisoner and warden. An additional expressed goal is to foster team-building and cooperation among managers who have shared the common experience of the seminar.

Aspen Institute seminars undoubtedly influenced ARCO's own Executive Continuum since its chairman Robert O. Anderson inherited Paepcke's leadership role at the Aspen Institute and has guided the development for 20 years. The Executive Continuum is held on ARCO's Santa Barbara, California, campus for all upper-grade executives. These sessions discuss corporate management and future plans and stress the larger societal issues that affect the company in U.S. and foreign operations. The goal is to increase individual awareness and "to stimulate the desire to acquire a broader and more far-ranging knowledge" of the business and its various socio-political environments. Agenda items in the ARCO program include: Public Affairs, Politics and You, Computing Technology and the Executive, Technological Future, Ethics and Decision Making, International Geo-political Perspectives, Human Resource Systems, and Visions of the Future. Hopefully, besides gaining insights, managers will be motivated to get out and participate in public affairs in their own communities.

IBM has a long list of continuing learning opportunities outside the company for its corporate leaders and has charted objectives and curriculum on a grid that indicates breadth of conceptual concerns.

TABLE 1

IBM OUT-COMPANY PROGRAMS

	GENERAL MANAGEMENT	LEADERSHIP	PUBLIC AFFAIRS	HUMANITIES
OBJECTIVES	Broaden functional managers	Increase executive understanding of interpersonal relationships	Provide exposure to federal government operations and major policy issues	Provide perspective on man, society, and values
CURRICULUM	Finance, Economics, Organizational behavior, Management science, Corporate strategy	Conflict, Stress, Organizational change, Behavior, Psychology	Business-government relations, Governmental process and Leadership problems	Science, Philosophy, Religion, Literature, Culture, Governance
AVERAGE PROGRAM LENGTH	4 weeks (Range: 2 weeks to 1 year)	1 week (Range: 1 to 3 weeks)	1 week	2 weeks (Range: 1½ to 6 weeks)

These examples of executive education are from flagship corporations with enlightened leadership that is committed to education and training and willing to pay for it.

Seymour Lusterman has reported on what is happening more generally in one specific area of corporate training—the public affairs aspect of managerial competence.[4] From a survey of 176 firms among *Fortune's* top 1,300 industrials and nonindustrials, he sums up: A marked increase in public affairs activities has occurred in recent years, and most executives expect their companies to increase attention in the years ahead. Nearly one-half of the corporations provided courses, seminars, or workshops either in-house or outside to develop such competence. More than one-half brought in people with special affairs knowledge to address and meet with managers.

Although some 50 percent of the companies in his study offer courses or special sessions, Lusterman concludes, nevertheless, that few are really "seriously and systematically addressing the question of how to improve current managerial capabilities for public affairs and provide for the future." Some say a great deal of change is needed in companies' development attitudes and, typically, blame top management, particularly in large industrial firms.

One other issue. Most corporate education programs separate training for management from technical personnel training. Such a division reflects the differences in the nature of training for each group. But the separation can also narrow the vision and lead to inadequacy. An employee may, in fact, require *both* technical *and* managerial training. Engineers moving into management ordinarily receive general manager development training, but the reverse is not so often the case. There is an urgent need for general managers who understand the latest technological developments, their implications, and their application in manufacturing processes.

The need to cross those lines is well stated by James P. Baughman, Director of Management Education for the General Electric Company. Baughman focuses specifically on the context of America's business schools and their lack of responsiveness to actual business needs:

There is a great deal of catching up to do on computer-based information systems. . . . There is vast illiteracy on business school faculties in these areas, not only just in the mechanics but in terms of their implications. We find ourselves in a "kind of no-man's land in the curricula between the engineering and science people who really have the technical ability but can't teach it in a management context and the people who have management sensitivity but really can't link it up with the technical know how."[5]

The same problem is pointed out even more sharply by Yoshi Tsurumi in a comparison of Japanese and U.S. executives in some 20 to 24 competitive industries such as semiconductors, computers, consumer electronics, steel, autos, chemicals, pharmaceuticals, industrial equipment, and processed foods. In comments titled "Too Many U.S. Managers are Technologically Illiterate," he says that their business school education tends "to make them aloof from the factory floor and from the human beings who are involved in the day-to-day tasks of making products." They lack familiarity with their whole organization, so he asks: "Is it any wonder that they are drawn to legal or financial solutions rather than technical or human ones?"[6]

Although ethical issues have been added to the curriculum since Derek Bok's criticisms some five years ago, Harvard's Business School still remains devoted to its celebrated case study method—which does not appear to have many cases from rapidly advancing frontiers of high tech. A student observes that the method stays at least a few years behind the times "because you can't wait for a good case on robotics to come along."[7]

Looking at business schools' catalogs is not reassuring. There are, however, joint degree programs such as those at Columbia and the Wharton School in which students may take both an MBA and the M.S. in Engineering in four or five terms. Corporations would be well advised to look closely at these graduates; they might help to solve the problem of crossing lines.

Meanwhile, corporate catalogs listing courses for management give little explicit evidence of concern with teaching technological developments to managers, but perhaps it is just assumed, at least in high-tech firms, that

70

such expertise will be acquired by the time managers reach top levels. In the "Out Company Executive Programs" for one multinational firm, one- to four-week sessions are regularly scheduled with leading universities for advanced technical programs. But these courses are typically for managers already in technical assignments. This tends to increase professional specialization for top technical personnel while, in contrast, programs for other top management executives tend toward broadening concepts and understanding. So, the dichotomy persists.

TECHNICAL AND SCIENTIFIC STUDY

Overall, management has had the lion's share of attention in the corporate curriculum. As one company officer put it, "Why not? Management makes the decision about who gets what and how much." But he quickly added that the scales were tipping in the new knowledge-intensive industries. Technological personnel are receiving ever greater attention, and there is a marked increase in the numbers of advanced training courses offered. The day of the engineer and the scientist has dawned.

Technical and scientific training runs the gamut from high school-level subject matter to the most advanced post-doctoral courses: from apprentice trade programs and on-the-job learning to courses on Principles of Radar, Pastel and Earth Targets Sensitometry, or international banking operations, and investments. The complicated acronyms for technical processes carry little meaning for general readers and course titles become merely confusing.

A few observations, however, may indicate the present state of affairs in some types of firms and presage developments. Automation of the banking industry, for example, has led to a tremendous multiplication of training courses for keyboard operation, word processing concepts, and technical training for specific machines. Manufacturers Hanover—clearly not banking on one machine type alone—trains for Digital, Wang, Xerox, and IBM equipment.

Before the trend toward compatible software started, companies were completely dependent on their own personnel and on professional advisers-instructors from equipment manufacturers to set up their records and information processing systems. To a great extent, this is still the case and may remain so because of differences in company policies. An entire work force is being reeducated to operate technical systems. This is not only true for the banking industry, but also for many service companies in retailing, food merchandising, hotel service, insurance, and health care, which have their own complicated monitoring and delivery techniques. Automation has brought a whole new course category to technical training catalogs.

Beyond the educational demands created by technology in service companies, there is also the need for high level training in the inventing companies themselves. Each new product calls for another round of training for its applied use. Companies dependent on engineering and scientific research for their very existence must provide a most extensive range of training, both in-house and outside, if they intend to stay in the race. Basic training for personnel is essential to maintain an ample pool from which to select those top, so-called sophisticated, few who will invent the future.

General Electric began its famous three-year basic engineering course—the ABC—in 1923 and offered an in-house certificate upon completion. Now, in affiliation with various universities, employees can transfer credit toward masters' and doctorate degrees. The program's success led Honeywell, not long ago, to send its employees to General Electric's ABC program. Courses offered are in basic engineering, so GE "is not concerned with sharing company secrets."[8] More such cooperative training arrangements are developing among corporations.

Concurrently GE—with some 380,000 employees in 360 locations worldwide—offers courses at every level of technical advancement, including basics in nuclear engineering, electronic hardware technology and fast reactor technology. From the Nuclear Energy Business Operations, located in Silicon Valley, GE engineers go to Stanford University's Honors Cooperative Program and other technical graduate programs in the area—along with engineers from Hewlett-Packard and many Valley high-tech companies. Where new knowledge is predicated on higher mathematical and scientific skills, university courses may be appropriate, but for industrial engineering laboratories involved in company problems, on-site

72

courses may prove more directly profitable to the company. Keeping the options flexible, the corporation offers both opportunities.

Technical personnel are frequently encouraged by their companies to participate in their respective professional societies. Faculty listings for in-house company institutes often include papers delivered at professional meetings along with academic credentials and books published—criteria that may be included in a conventional college or university catalog.

Upgrading technical personnel is a never-ending process starting with on-the-job training and basic remedial work. In this respect, course catalogs change little over the years; big changes come in advanced graduate courses. Among top-ranking industrials the prevailing opinion is that educational opportunities will continue to expand.[9] Significant reduction would, they are convinced, surely erode the industry's top-ranking position.

SALES, SERVICE, AND CUSTOMER TRAINING

Sales and service typically has its own educational arm in large corporations alongside management and technical training. Here, too, expansion and change are keys to the competitive marketplace and in determining the bottom line. Training for sales and service has long been a part of company education, but as the economy shifted toward information industries—particularly those that are termed "knowledge-intensive" and driven by high technology—both the nature and amount of such training were bound to change. And, this is exactly what has happened.

No company has placed greater emphasis on sales training and customer support than IBM; it has become the leviathan of marketing. Starting from his belief that salesmen are made, not born, and that "there is no saturation point in education," founding father Thomas A. Watson, Sr. established the first formal training program for salesmen in the tabulating machine division in 1916. That same year he established an Education Department and, two years later, the first formal customer class for key punch operators in Springfield, Massachusetts.[10] He also held the credo—no doubt oft repeated—that it was not a product until it was sold!

At IBM, training for marketing and technical skills went hand-in-hand;

personnel in both fields learned components of machines and wiring electronic boards in the early days. Sales techniques continued their close link to systems engineers' training, with additional emphasis on public speaking and communications skills. Recently, the two job functions have been re-analyzed, and training has been made more specific for each. Technical complexity and multiple applications force increased specialization.

The microelectronic revolution of the 1960s, and the availability of computers that could do increasingly clever things at ever lower prices, sparked more training for both employees and customers. Demand and need led to charging customers for their education and no longer absorbing it in the product price. As new products appear and systems emerge to perform more complicated tasks, those involved in marketing inevitably require continuous training.

In 1979 "service and information" industries accounted for 72 percent of U.S. employees compared to 25 percent in manufacturing and 3 percent in agriculture.[11] Classified as information industries are computers, microelectronic components, instruments, telecommunications and other information technologies, software, services, new biogenetic companies and pharmaceuticals, chemical companies, aerospace, and so on. Each of these industries is heavily dependent on *knowledge* and makes extensive use of the sciences and technology.[12]

Little imagination is needed to see the impact on education and training within such companies, and on customers who must use the new products. One business teaches another business, teaches office and technical personnel in many other firms, and programs the "new gadgets" to perform particular company-specific functions for the client. The training web becomes endless. Furthermore, as the product goes into homes, the role of business as educational provider extends to the American public and world as training is carried to citizens abroad. Digital Equipment Corporation's customer support, for example, includes maintainance, software support, and training services—backed by 18,000 support personnel in 39 countries. Digital's training curriculum offers more than 300 courses in 17 languages. The courses are self-paced, interactive computer-based, and regular classes are also held at customer sites.

GENERAL EDUCATION

The full curricular spectrum, particularly as seen through the employee's eyes, requires one more large and rather general category. It could as well be called personal enrichment, or growth, or individual career development. A common corporate philosophy for education programs is to promote *personal* fulfillment along with professional development; it recognizes the faint, almost imperceptible line that separates personal growth from professional or career advancement. At Polaroid, for example, the department under Human Resource Development is labeled "Education and Career Planning" while other departments cover management, corporate skills, and organization development. Such distinctions are necessarily rather arbitrary because courses can be suitable to more than one category and are sometimes listed in several. Another example—difficult to categorize—is Dow Chemical's PLAN or Personal Learning As Needed.

There is a wide variety of courses commonly available to both hourly (non-exempt) and salaried and professional (exempt) personnel. They cut across levels and types of employment. Orientation courses, for example, fall into this category—company-wide and introducing corporate policies and goals, benefits and educational opportunities with career counseling. Safety courses may also be found here, especially in large manufacturing firms, public utilities, and transportation.

Many of the general courses are in communications: effective writing for letters, memos, technical matters; interpersonal relations and cross-cultural communications. Many courses include self-assessment, personal financial planning, logic, and so forth. Basic instruction in secondary school-level work could be placed here, and high school equivalency exams are made available.

There is an increasing number of courses and programs termed "pre-retirement" since Hewlett-Packard started its pre-retirement program 15 years ago. Some of the courses have intriguing titles like Polaroid's "The Process of Aging: Myths of Productivity" that addresses misconceptions which, according to the course description, "have a negative impact on our self-image and perspective on work. . . . Participants explore myths associated with ages 30, 40, 55, 62, and 70; learn new perspectives on the aging process; and explore methods to support the aging worker's interests, motivation, growth and productivity." The course just described is listed for both management and general education.

New corporate courses are given on request of divisions or local units, usually after an assessment of need, but since employee motivation and morale are major assets, "need" may enjoy a rather broad definition. The individual in an enlightened workplace may choose among foreign languages, Psychology in Industry, Sociological Impact of Technology, American History and Government, and many others. A rather unique course is Kimberly-Clark's special course on "Images of Business in Literature" that includes works such as *Babbitt*, *Walden*, and *Death of a Salesman*. Further, if the employee elects to use the company's tuition refund plan, he or she can get a liberal education by combining studies in house and outside—which leads to the next issue.

OVERLAP WITH THE EDUCATIONAL ESTABLISHMENT

Recalling sample course titles suggests both areas of overlap and some direct duplication between the corporate education system and the traditional system of schools, colleges and universities. Since the two systems have developed in parallel, the present situation has obviously not come about by intent. Indeed, over the years, companies have tried to influence school and college curricula to obtain better workers, but efforts have been rather ineffective and, sometimes, misguided. Companies have, therefore, simultaneously continued to develop their own training programs.

Corporations are certainly not deliberately, or altruistically, in the business of education for their employees; they are in production of goods and services. But, to do this well, they have been forced—often reluctantly—to educate. They have responded to *need* and demand, primarily to remedy training deficiencies and fill gaps. Implied is an indictment of the schools, particularly in the areas of language and computation. Extensive course listings of basic, effective writing, reading, arithmetic and mathematics, communications skills, presenting a paper, and logical expression should not have to be so essential and prevalent in corporate education catalogs. Recent reforms proposed for American high schools stress the importance of doing a better job in those same subjects for which industry now gives compensatory training.

The indictment, however, extends beyond secondary schools. One might expect that with the growing presence of college graduates in the work force, remedial and basic courses in industry would decline, but such is not the case. Beyond basics, more and more companies are teaching analytical skills and critical thinking, conceptual bases for transferable knowledge, foreign languages, psychology and sociology, economics, college algebra, physics, and other courses in science and technology. These studies—clearly the domain of colleges and universities—should not need to be duplicated in corporate classrooms, at least not for college graduates.

The key difference in the two systems, however, is theory vs. application, and this distinction is mentioned repeatedly by the corporations that have started their own degree-granting colleges and institutes. Why shouldn't colleges use more practical problems to display a theory's applicability? Would such an adjustment destroy the essence of a theory, or a field of study for that matter? New simulation techniques may make it simpler and easier to demonstrate practical uses, if faculty learn the techniques. But, college faculties generally are not noted for their eagerness to change, or even to develop new courses. That is a harsh judgment, one expressed by a considerable number of critics—not just in the corporate world.

In a pointedly critical document, General Electric, in its 1979 course description, printed the comparison between a GE Advanced Course and instruction at a traditional college shown in Table 2.[13] In fairness, the unique purposes of the two systems account for some of the disparity. Corporations march to a different drummer—production and customer. On other points, however, criticisms of higher education instruction reveal questionable weaknesses and deserve consideration.

To restrict overlapping education efforts, traditional institutions might well reexamine their curriculum and requirements for graduation to accomplish more effectively their own professed purposes. Faculty may be reminded that subjects can be taught as preparation for many future careers—not only for the perpetuation of their profession.

But not all overlap is due to industry's attempt to overcome the in-

TABLE 2

DIFFERENCES BETWEEN ADVANCED COURSE
AND COLLEGE EDUCATION

COLLEGE	ADVANCED COURSE
1. Teacher-Student Relationship	1. Supervisor-Engineer
2. Teacher knows all	2. Supervisor knows problem
3. Learn for education's sake	3. Learn to get an answer
4. Work exercises to learn principles	4. Solve problems to get results
5. Show what you know	5. Show what the customer needs
6. Include scratchwork	6. Edit for clear reading
7. Skip arithmetic if pressed	7. Numerical result needed
8. Understanding most important	8. Results are important
9. Cooperation forbidden	9. Cooperation encouraged
10. Student behavior	10. Professional behavior

adequacies of school and college graduates. It also reflects the initiative colleges take to offer more career-oriented courses in order to attract students: for example, the recent growth in computer science courses and, earlier, general business courses. Undoubtedly, companies welcome these graduates for certain positions, but similar courses are still deemed necessary in the corporate curriculum. Thus, as many companies become more like colleges, in turn, colleges become more like the corporate campus.

Some overlap between college and industry education is inevitable, of course, since teaching purposes differ. Corporate education may be seen as adding diversity to America's educational opportunities—long viewed as a strength. Certainly the corporate system adds rich opportunities for adults to learn. But as the corporate educational system grows, colleges may feel more competition from business classrooms. Companies are offering both wages and a variety of educational options. Today it is possible to both take a job and continue studies gradually for a degree. Credits are more easily transferred and business has more direct alignments with higher education institutions to encourage the pattern. Everyone wins, but the student and the corporation may be winning more than colleges and universities because increasing numbers of courses are offered in house by the corporation.

QUALITY OF CORPORATE COURSES

A corporate classroom can be quite impressive if judged by intensity of instruction, high student motivation, well-organized presentation by the teacher and a course outline with clearly stated goals. Further, if the corporate course is programmed for self-instruction with or without computer assistance it may have these same attributes—minus the trainer's live presence, of course. But that is purely subjective evaluation. If, however, quality is defined as what is acceptable for academic credit by traditional higher education, or if corporate courses are compared specifically with those of established institutions, the judgment may differ and carry more weight and credence.

Some companies that have strong in-house programs have worked out transfer arrangements with higher education institutions, thus showing academic acceptance for work taken at the company. Credit is given, for example, for some NCR courses at various colleges located near company facilities in different parts of the country. Dana University has liaison with the University of Toledo for a master's degree in engineering and with Bowling Green State University for MBAs. For many years Union College in Schenectady, New York, has credited General Electric's courses toward an advanced degree in power systems engineering. And among IBM's many collaborative plans, direct ties exist between their Systems Research Institute and the School of Advanced Technology at the State University of New York's Binghamton graduate center. Employee-students co-register and transfer 15 credits for the degree—the same number commonly accepted between universities. About 30 percent of a class of 130 to 145 students take advantage of the plan. SRI annually runs three classes of ten weeks each and offers 75 courses in seven curricular areas.

Similar alliances between corporations and specific campuses operate on a one-to-one basis all across the country; companies know employees may want academic recognition, and it fits company goals for higher training of personnel. So, employers pay the bill for continuing education, according to corporate policies, and usually ask a rather high grade average for reimbursement. Since studies done in house are awarded credit by the cooperating college or university, quality may be assumed to be at least equal to that of the higher education institution.

Some corporations are also joining a nationwide Program on Noncollegiate Sponsored Instruction (PONSI) that evaluates specific corporate courses and recommends academic credit at appropriate levels. Evaluation, a formal procedure, asks the company trainer to submit forms explaining course objectives, methods, syllabus, qualifications for participants and instructors, hours, location, dates of instruction, and most important—techniques for judging student performance. Subject matter specialists from colleges and universities then visit the site for one or more days to see the class in action and talk with those involved. Credit may be recommended for some number of semester hours at lower or upper division levels of college work or for graduate degree studies.

Of nearly 200 noncollegiate organizations and a total of 2,200 courses evaluated by the American Council on Education's PONSI, about one-half are private corporations. Under the New York State Regents' PONSI (the two programs started together in 1974 and separated in 1977), some 150 organizations participate and another 1,500 courses have been evaluated. Generally the lists of the two programs are distinct, but occasionally a company like GE or Xerox participates in both. Other companies cooperating include AT&T, Control Data, Dana Corporation, Dresser Industries, NCR Corporation, Westinghouse, and many smaller firms.

PONSI evaluation is probably the best yardstick of quality that exists for corporate classrooms. Why do corporations bother with such academic evaluation and pay for it at a cost of $2,500 to $3,750, plus travel and lodging for a one- or two-day visit to evaluate one course? More than helping their employees' to earn their first or next degree, there may be prestige involved and, perhaps, curiosity about the quality of their courses. Corporations also want to be sure the instructor, content, and pupil per-

80

formance are good; they welcome "objective" outside evaluation. Quality is no more uniform in corporate classrooms than in college classrooms.

At the same time, not all employers are overwhelmed with admiration for academic degrees. One executive of a very large, educationally sensitive firm said, "I could not care less about academic credentials that are below my standards for performance on the job." Nevertheless, he bet on odds and encouraged employees to continue their studies for degrees. There just might be some learning relevant to their work.

Still, most corporate executives are supportive of colleges and universities and reflect the desire to strengthen them. Many—with extensive education systems of their own—state firmly that they have no interest either in granting their own degrees or in competing with the educational establishment.

PONSI's academic evaluating role took a new turn when the American Council on Education set up a National Registry of Credit Recommendations. This new service establishes a "transcript" for the employee-student which shows courses passed, describes course content, and lists the number of credits recommended. The transcript is valuable in two ways: first, to facilitate the granting of credit by the collegiate institution in which the student may wish to enroll, and second, to provide for the worker a record of the training he or she has received that may influence a job transfer or promotion.

Over 11,000 employees had entered the National Registry by 1984. It is indeed a mammoth undertaking when one thinks of the millions of workers who eventually may wish to participate in the national educational information bank.

The American Council's PONSI has further extended its scope to include evaluation of vendors' courses and those using new technologies. This opens another very large market for evaluation and credit recommendations; it will also serve the corporations that may use the vendors' courses. Evaluation procedures are similar to those used for more orthodox classrooms and quality controls include administering examinations.

Xerox has its own counselors in regional offices to help employees transfer the recommended credit into the New York Regents' external degree program—a nontraditional approach that is more open to credit acceptance than many older institutions. A more typical experience, however, is that of Consolidated Edison Company of New York. A company executive reports:

> We have been a strong supporter of the Noncollegiate Sponsored Instruction Program of the University of the State of New York [The Regent's Program]. Most of our management courses have been approved for college credit, but we have had great difficulty in obtaining cooperation from local institutions to grant such credits. This seems to be a continuing problem which both discourages the students from attempting to gain credit and it discourages our staff from having the courses qualify for credit.

Facing similar resistance from colleges, Mountain Bell Training and Education Center in Colorado wrote the colleges in their region, described their courses (38 had credit recommendations), and asked whether the institution would be receptive or not. Answers were printed for employees to see immediately which colleges were inclined to consider credits earned in company courses. Within a few months almost 100 students had a total of 254 credits accepted by colleges, and they were on their way to degree work. Incidentally, by getting their courses accepted for credit, Mountain Bell figures it saved $30,000 in tuition reimbursement.

Finally, the quality of instruction in the corporate classroom may also be measured by comparing it directly with the same subject being taught in a regular collegiate institution. Jeanette S. Baker takes this approach. She lists courses and requirements in exhaustive detail for General Motors Institute's four bachelor programs and compares them with programs at Arizona State University, Illinois Institute of Technology, the University of Arizona, New Jersey Institute of Technology, and other institutions.

Comparisons reveal more similarities than differences in courses, but GMI, surprisingly, asks for more humanities and social sciences; requires composition of technical reports and scientific articles, oral as well as written; and is more concerned with management decisions. Overall, GMI has more requirements, fewer electives, and requires a problem-oriented thesis for graduation. Its program is a year longer and combines work experience with study. Nevertheless, GMI's technical courses bear strong resemblance to their counterparts on college campuses. Baker concludes that it is the "unexpected breadth" of general education at GMI that stands out when compared to technical degree programs at traditional institutions.[14]

The corporate curriculum is extensive for management, technical professionals, sales representatives and service personnel. Company courses offer opportunities for general education and basic remedial work that can earn the high school diploma for some and can lead to more advanced degrees for others in the work force. Duplication of courses given by the traditional education system asks for careful consideration by the establishment. Differences in the purposes of the two systems do not fully account for the overlap. In many instances, industry's need is completely consistent with established education's goals, so it challenges the regular classroom to improve.

Corporate education, on its side too, has problems. Its classrooms do not take full advantage of newer teaching techniques although delivery systems circle the globe. Corporations also have to watch out for self-imposed limitations as in-house programs proliferate; they may need more outside courses from vendors and colleges and universities to broaden the point of view in classrooms and to emphasize objective opinions. Leaders in industrial training are using these various options to keep their classrooms open, but others are not.

In addition, corporate content for managers' courses is under fire from some quarters: Managers are seen as "technologically illiterate" for industries that are adjusting to the new wave of revolutionary processes and products. Regardless of corrections needed, the corporate curriculum is making a major contribution to adult learning. And it is not only for career advancement, it is also for personal enrichment. There are many citizens who have learned and enjoyed the benefits of teaching in corporate classrooms.

CHAPTER V

Corporate Colleges with Academic Degrees

A NEW DEVELOPMENT on the scene of business and education is the growing number of corporate colleges, institutes, or universities that grant their own academic degrees. It is the Rand Ph.D., the Wang or Arthur D. Little Master of Science degree. No longer the purview of established educational institutions alone, accredited academic degrees are being awarded increasingly by companies and industries that have created their own separate institutions and successfully passed the same educational hurdles used to accredit traditional higher education.

If this is startling news to the higher education establishment, just consider a recent prediction by *U.S. News and World Report.* In the next 50 years, the magazine suggests:

> Industry, for one, will become much more involved in education and job training. Hundreds of corporations will grant degrees, most often in high technology, science, and engineering, where state-of-the-art equipment and research will surpass that on most campuses.[1]

Projecting ahead only *five* years, five industrial corporations say they are definitely planning to start at least nine more degree-granting programs in management, semiconductor design, systems engineering, and business administration. And, on the basis of their statements, it is also anticipated that eight corporations will offer a combined total of 19 college-level degree programs by 1988.[2] With this rate of growth, it may not be too fanciful to foresee 100—if not hundreds—of corporate degree programs in the next 50 years.

The newest entry—the National Technological University—is a space-age model for the immediate future. By fall 1985, instruction will go by satellite to many corporate classrooms. At off hours of evening and night, courses can be recorded for use in various time zones at the convenience of students, and electronic mail will be used for feedback. Teleconferencing for students and faculty will start in 1985 with video out and telephone back.

NTU operates from a central office—no campus necessary—at Fort Collins, Colorado. Without residency requirements and with course work registered centrally, the mobile career engineer can finally earn NTU's degree, which takes "the bureaucratic confusion out of advanced engineering education."

In the fall of '84 two complete curricula started by videotape in Computer Engineering and Engineering Management for the NTU Master of Science degree; the next three programs for the M.S. in Electrical Engineering and in Mechanical and Industrial Engineering (with concentrations on manufacturing) will "get off the ground" soon.

Queries have come from Mexico and Canada about enrollment. Although delivery can be managed, NTU's President Lionel Baldwin and the distinguished trustees from corporations and universities are considering the legality and propriety of an American university awarding degrees in other countries. It is a provocative issue posed by the ever extending power of communication. Meanwhile, some 500 employee-students from 30 different sites in the United States enrolled in 1984 for six courses.

A model in more ways than its use of communications, NTU represents a merger of corporate interests with universities' resources and federal government concerns. The corporations, needing more advanced, high-level training for technical personnel, contributed time and money to support the establishment of the university. IBM, Westinghouse, Hewlett-Packard, Digital Equipment, NCR, RCA and Control Data Corporation were among the first 12 contributing companies, and they are happy with the results. As one corporate official gleefully exclaimed, "The universities are waiting to sign our dance card!"

From the major research universities in the Association for Media-Based Continuing Education for Engineers came the course development—

86

a wide choice from experts in specific technical areas. Students have direct contact with some of the best engineering professors from the 15 participating universities. The United States Department of Defense budgeted at $126,000 for the first year as the beginning of a cost reimbursable contract to offer advanced instruction for the Army, Navy, and Air Force. NTU, in effect, is a round-up of talent, pooled and made available for classrooms in corporations and the Armed Forces.

This meteoric new university is unusual, even among the motley group of institutions called *corporate colleges*. At present, 18 such corporate educational institutions have been discovered, largely by chance.[3] No special nationwide registry of such institutions exists as yet; some are listed in the official Higher Education Directory, but others are not. A check of the institutions shows ten missing, primarily the newer ones. Although they are an odd assortment of types and hybrids that challenge clear definition, they all give academic degrees and most significantly, their number is increasing.

First, their heritage. In a pattern that is similar to some of the nation's more traditional institutions, corporate colleges often began with the inspiration of single individuals. Dr. An Wang and Mr. John Northrop created institutions that bear their names. Dr. Solomon S. Huebner of the University of Pennsylvania started the American College of Life Underwriters known today as the American College. His name is remembered in the largest of their programs under the Huebner School. Other founding fathers are discovered in the history of each place.

In addition to the guiding hand and dedicated efforts of single individuals, major support also came from other sources that made their ideas a reality, that built the school. The American Graduate School of International Management is a good example. In 1946 the School was organized under the forceful leadership of General Barton Kyle Yount, head of the U.S. Army Air Force Training Command during World War II. Realizing that U.S. business was increasingly going to be internationally involved and that it was generally ill-prepared for work abroad, Yount marshalled resources to meet the challenge.

From the U.S. War Assets Administration he got the campus—a deactivated pilot training center called Thunderbird, located near Phoenix,

Arizona. At the same time, the first capital was provided by unsecured loans as a public service by Arizona Bank, Bankers Trust Company, Chase Manhattan, and others as well as the directors of the School. Banks, government, and the community came together to create a national graduate school for international studies and business careers. Some 30 leading corporations and financial institutions discussed frankly their worldwide personnel problems and the training they thought most needed—the groundwork for the pragmatic, people-oriented curriculum today.

Examining the 18 corporate education institutions in this report and the sources responsible for their development shows three general types of sponsors:

> *Individual business corporations.* Six were created or nurtured by the following companies: General Motors, Northrop Aircraft, MetriData Computing, Wang, McDonald's Corporation, and Bell and Howell.

> *Industrywide interest and concern* spawned six of the institutions. The textile mills of North America cooperatively established the Institute of Textile Technology. Insurance interests set up the College of Insurance in New York City and the American College in Pennsylvania. And Bostonian bankers encouraged the American Institute of Banking there to become accredited and offer the Associate Degree of Business Administration in Banking Studies. Corporations—generally classified as high-tech—joined to start the National Technological University. And banks, with help from government, made possible The American Graduate School of International Management.

> *Professional, research, and consulting organizations* have started six degree-granting institutes and programs: the Arthur D. Little Management Education Institute, the Rand Corporation's Graduate Institute, the American Management Association's Institute for Management Competency, the Industrial Management Institute of the Midwest Industrial Management Association, Massachusetts General Hospital Corporation's Institute of Health Professions, and the Boston Architectural Center that now gives the bachelor's degree in architecture.

88

TABLE 3

CORPORATE COLLEGES

INSTITUTION	SPONSOR AND HISTORY	STATUS	DATE ESTABLISHED AND DATE DEGREE APPROVED BY STATE	NONGOVERNMENTAL ACCREDITATION	DEGREES AWARDED
AMERICAN COLLEGE *Bryn Mawr, PA*	National Association of Life Underwriters Began as American College of Life Underwriters. Name legally changed in 1976	Independent Nonprofit	Est. 1927 M.S.F.S. Degree 1976 M.S.M. Degree 1982	Middle States Association of Colleges and Schools	M.S. in: • Financial Services • Management
AMERICAN GRADUATE SCHOOL OF INTERNATIONAL MANAGEMENT *Glendale, AZ*	Banks Individuals and U.S. Government Began as American Institute of Foreign Trade. Changed to Thunderbird Graduate School of International Management in 1968, and to present name in 1973	Independent Nonprofit	Est. 1946 Degree 1946	North Central Association of Colleges and Schools	Master of International Management

TABLE 3 (*cont.*)

INSTITUTION	SPONSOR AND HISTORY	STATUS	DATE ESTABLISHED AND DATE DEGREE APPROVED BY STATE	NONGOVERN-MENTAL ACCREDITATION	DEGREES AWARDED
AMERICAN INSTITUTE OF BANKING AT BOSTON *Boston, MA*	American Institute of Banking at Boston First of National Institutes of Banking to grant degrees	Independent Nonprofit	Est. 1909 Degree 1979	New England Association of Schools and Colleges (Candidacy Status)	Associate Degree of Business Administration in Banking Studies
ARTHUR D. LITTLE MANAGEMENT EDUCATION INSTITUTE *Cambridge, MA*	Arthur D. Little, Inc.	Integral to Corporation, Proprietary*	Est. 1964 Degrees 1973	New England Association of Schools and Colleges	M.S. in: • Administration • Management
BOSTON ARCHITECTURAL CENTER SCHOOL OF ARCHITECTURE *Boston, MA*	Boston Architectural Center Began as Boston Architectural Club in 1889. Informal evening courses for persons employed	Independent Nonprofit	Est. 1944 Degree 1979	National Architectural Accrediting Board	Bachelor of Architecture

Institution	Affiliation / History	Control	Established / Degrees	Accreditation	Degrees Offered
DEVRY INSTITUTES OF TECHNOLOGY *Chicago, IL* — 10 OTHER LOCATIONS IN U.S. AND CANADA	Bell & Howell Company DeVry, Inc. The Chicago Institute was first. All grant degrees except 2 in Canada and 1 in U.S. Became Bell and Howell Education Group renamed DeVry, Inc. in August, 1983	Integral to Corporation, Proprietary	Est. 1931 A.A.S. Degree 1957 B.A. Degree 1969	North Central Association of Colleges and Schools; National Association of Trade and Technical Schools; Accreditation Board for Engineering and Technology	B.A. and A.A.S. in: • Electronics Engineering Technology • Computer Information Systems
G.M.I. ENGINEERING AND MANAGEMENT INSTITUTE *Flint, MI*	General Motors Corporation. Began as night school. G.M. adopted in 1926. Became independent in 1982.	Independent Nonprofit	Est. 1919 Degree 1945	North Central Association of Colleges and Schools; Accreditation Board for Engineering and Technology	Bachelor of: • Mechanical Engineering • Industrial Engineering • Electrical Engineering • Industrial Management Master of Manufacturing Management

TABLE 3 (*cont.*)

INSTITUTION	SPONSOR AND HISTORY	STATUS	DATE ESTABLISHED AND DATE DEGREE APPROVED BY STATE	NONGOVERNMENTAL ACCREDITATION	DEGREES AWARDED
INDUSTRIAL MANAGEMENT INSTITUTE *Westchester, IL*	Midwest Industrial Management Association	Integral to Corporation Nonprofit	Est. 1982 Operating Authority 1982**	North Central Association of Colleges and Schools (Application in Process)	A.A.S. in Industrial Management and Supervision
INSTITUTE OF MANAGEMENT COMPETENCY *New York, NY San Francisco, CA*	American Management Associations Outgrowth of 5-year Behavioral Research Study of Managerial Skills	Integral to Corporation Nonprofit	Est. 1980 Degree 1982 (Cal.) (Awaited in N.Y.)	Middle States Association of Colleges and Schools (Application Planned)	Master of Management
INSTITUTE OF TEXTILE TECHNOLOGY *Charlottesville, VA*	Cooperative Program of Textile Industry in U.S. and Canada	Independent Nonprofit	Est. 1944 Degree 1947	Southern Association of Colleges and Schools (Application Pending)	M.S. and Ph.D. in Textile Technology
MGH INSTITUTE OF HEALTH PROFESSIONS *Boston, MA*	Massachusetts General Hospital Corporation Outgrowth of Reevaluation of Teaching Programs	Integral to Corporation Nonprofit	Est. 1980 Degree 1977	New England Association of Schools and Colleges (Candidacy Status)	M.S. in: • Dietetics • Nursing • Physical Therapy • Speech-Language Pathology

Institution	Type	Affiliation / History	Established	Accreditation	Degrees Offered
McDONALD'S MANAGEMENT INSTITUTE *Oak Brook, IL*	Integral to Corporation Proprietary*	McDonald's Corporation Hamburger University	Est. 1961 Operating Authority 1982**	North Central Association of Colleges and Schools (Application Planned)	A.A.S. in Business Management
NATIONAL TECHNOLOGICAL UNIVERSITY central office *Fort Collins, CO*	Independent Nonprofit	Major Business Corporations*** U.S. Government and AMCEE Developed from courses offered by universities in the Association for Media-Based Continuing Education for Engineers	Est. 1984 Degree 1984	North Central Association of Colleges and Schools (Application Pending) Courses approved by participating universities	M.S. in: • Computer Engineering • Engineering Management • Electrical Engineering • Industrial Engineering • Mechanical Engineering
NORTHROP UNIVERSITY *Inglewood, CA*	Independent Nonprofit	Northrop Corporation Began as Northrop Aeronautical Institute, a division of the corporation. Became independent in 1958 as Northrop Institute of Technology. In 1975 became Northrop University	Est. 1942 Degree 1958	Western Association of Schools and Colleges Accreditation Board for Engineering and Technology Committee of Bar Examiners of the State Bar of California	B.S. and M.S. in: • Engineering (Aerospace Electronics, etc.) • Business Administration M.S. in Systems and Logistics Management and Technology Masters in: • Taxation • Procurement Acquisition Management J.D.

TABLE 3 (*cont.*)

INSTITUTION	SPONSOR AND HISTORY	STATUS	DATE ESTABLISHED AND DATE DEGREE APPROVED BY STATE	NONGOVERNMENTAL ACCREDITATION	DEGREES AWARDED
RAND GRADUATE INSTITUTE *Santa Monica, CA*	Rand Corporation	Integral to Corporation Nonprofit	Est. 1970 Degree 1970	Western Association of Schools and Colleges	Ph.D. in Policy Analysis
THE COLLEGE OF INSURANCE *New York, NY* WESTERN DIVISION *Los Angeles, CA*	Insurance Society of New York Began as School of Insurance	Independent Nonprofit	Est. 1947 Degree 1962 Western Division 1979 (Diploma in Risk and Insurance)	Middle States Association of Colleges and Schools	M.B.A. and B.B.A. with major in Insurance B.S. in Actuarial Science Associate in Occupational Studies
WANG INSTITUTE OF GRADUATE STUDIES *Tyngsboro, MA*	Dr. An Wang and Wang Laboratories, Inc. Other corporations joined in early support	Independent Nonprofit	Est. 1979 Degree 1979	New England Association of Schools and Colleges (Candidacy Status)	Master of Software Engineering

WATTERSON COLLEGE MAIN CAMPUS *Louisville, KY* 2 OTHER LOCATIONS	Jostens, Inc.**** Began as College of Computer Sciences, became MetriData Institute. Changed to Watterson College in 1973 as part of MetriData Education Systems. Purchased by Jostens in 1983	Integral to Corporation Proprietary	Est. 1963 Degree 1973	Southern Association of Colleges and Schools Association of Independent Colleges and Schools Various Health Professional Organizations	Associate in: • Business Administration • Computer Programming • Fashion Merchandising • Medical Assistant • Medical Laboratory Technician • Secretarial Sciences

* Although these Institutes are subsidiary to profit-making corporations, they actually run on a nonprofit basis and are subsidized by the parent organization.

** The Illinois Board of Higher Education grants operating authority, after which the institutions return 3 years later for degree-granting authority.

*** IBM, Westinghouse, Hewlett-Packard, NCR, RCA, Control Data Corporation, Digital Equipment and others contributed. The Department of Defense for the Navy, Army, and Air Force budgeted at $126,000 for the beginning year as the first phase of a cost reimbursable contract.

**** Jostens, Inc., purchased MetriData Education Systems in December, 1983. Jostens is a manufacturer of college jewelry and insignia, olympic medals, and college sportswear. The company also owns four other colleges in Ohio and Indiana.

REFERENCE: Elizabeth Hawthorne, Patricia Libby, and Nancy Nash first identified 14 such institutions that were presented in ''The Emergence of Corporate Colleges,'' *The Journal of Continuing Education*, Fall 1983. This chart adds four, corrects and updates the list.

While corporate colleges differ in their origin and sponsorship, they were all started by incorporated organizations whose first purpose was not education. And there are characteristics that are shared as well as general trends that appear in their evolution. For example, two of these institutions sponsored by individual corporations primarily for their own employees have severed the parental connection and have become independent institutions serving a wider clientele.

General Motors Institute, originally a night school that was adopted by General Motors in the mid-twenties and developed into its main training center for engineers and managers, became an independent, freestanding institution in 1982. Today GMI operates as a nonprofit college, and the parent company is phasing out its $16 million underwriting for student support.

Some 200 companies, such as Gulf and Western, U.S. Steel, Bendix, Rockwell International, and the Ford Motor Company, are now sponsoring students, and only about half are currently units or parts of GM. The student body reflects the broader support base, and graduates will serve a larger number of different companies. In seeking funds to support itself, the Institute is extremely fortunate to have developed over the years a powerful alumni organization that could well be the envy of many small colleges.

Along with independence, GMI Engineering and Management Institute announced an extension of the curriculum to go beyond its five-year bachelor's program that combines work and study. The new master's degree program in manufacturing management will also go beyond the campus: using videotape, graduate studies are tailored for working engineers in the United States and abroad.

Similarly, Northrop University in California was started in the forties as a division of Northrop Aircraft, Inc. to train its personnel for the growing aircraft industry. The program eventually became the Northrop Aeronautical Institute, was divested by its parent company, and in 1958 emerged as a nonprofit entity with degree-granting authority. With an expanding curriculum and the mission broadened to serve the whole industry, it became Northrop University in 1975.

While its largest programs remain in technology and engineering es-

96

pecially for the aircraft business, Northrop University has added a School of Business and Management, a Law School awarding the J.D. degree, a Master's in Taxation, and a new master's level sequence in Procurement and Acquisition Management pertinent to industry-related government contracts. Started on campus, the new program is facing increasing demands from companies for the courses to be offered at locations convenient to their employees. Programs at Northrop University are accredited by the Western Association just as General Motors Institute is fully accredited by the North Central Association of Colleges and Schools.

The pattern of development among the older corporate institutions is generally along these lines. They have moved toward increasing independence, added academic degree work, broadened the curriculum and programs, and widened their clientele.

All 18 corporate institutions operate with what may be called an "open admissions" policy. They are, quite literally, open to all qualified persons *outside* the sponsoring corporation. While this is literally true, one exception requires notice: McDonald's Hamburger University basically serves only its own employees, but it admits students from its major supplier companies and has perhaps eight or so a year.

The important point is that these are not typically "in-house" educational programs for employees. The Rand, Wang, and Arthur D. Little institutes do not serve employees of their parent corporations; each admits students who meet their admission requirements from any college or university, any company, or from any country. Their graduates cannot expect employment by the sponsoring firm.

Some of these institutions draw students on an industrywide or professional basis as in the insurance and banking programs that serve personnel in those fields. The American Institute of Banking at Boston, for example, admits students from nonmember banks as well as member banks, and from the general public though there are very few of the latter. A high school diploma or equivalent is the basic requirement. The American College, initially serving the insurance field, has expanded to include persons from financial services, banking, investment, and attorneys working in such areas.

General Motors Institute and DeVry Institutes take qualified students directly from high schools; the Institute of Textile Technology is highly selective and searches out its students, awarding scholarships for master's and occasionally doctorate work in the sciences pertinent to textile development. Massachusetts General Hospital's Institute for Health Professions is open to any person qualified to pursue its master's program in nursing, dietetics, physical therapy, and speech-language pathology.

Many student bodies of the corporate colleges are international: the Rand Institute has 12 foreign students out of 60 in its Ph.D. program; Arthur D. Little's Institute originally was to train persons for management in developing countries, and so its student body was foreign, largely African. Lately, with interests broadening to include more from the developed world, students have been coming from Japan and more from the United States. Similarly, the American Graduate School of International Management has routinely had many foreign students; in an average semester 50 foreign countries may be represented—along with 45 states in the U.S.—in the current enrollment of more than 1,000 graduate students.

Courses from the American College in Pennsylvania are given in 25 countries abroad as well as throughout our country; General Motors Institute includes students from Canada and 15 other foreign countries. McDonald's Hamburger University, serving a worldwide corporation, has installed instant translation facilities for seven languages in the lecture hall and classrooms on its new campus at Oak Brook, Illinois. Northrop University, recognized around the world as a foremost center for aeronautical training, has special contract programs with foreign companies like the Saudi Arabian Airlines to train their technicians and other personnel. Two or three programs like this are in process all the time, exclusively for foreign students.

Although some of the older corporate institutions evolved toward broader based student bodies and added degree-granting status, all the newer ones—with the noted exception of McDonald's—started out with wider sources of clientele. The newer ones also began with degree-granting authority.

Of equal significance is the fact that the number of "corporate" degree institutions has been increasing. While General Motors Institute, The

American Graduate School of International Management, and the Institute of Textile Technology won their academic degree status in the 1940s, Northrop University in 1958, and the College of Insurance in New York and the DeVry Institute in Chicago in the 1960s, all the rest—12—gained degree status since 1970, and nine of these since 1977. Reasons for the marked increases are discussed later, after introducing the campuses and describing a selected few of the institutes and colleges in more detail to understand their nature and the type of academic work given.

In some places, one walks onto a campus that is like any small liberal arts college. Two- or three-storied buildings are grouped with joining walkways midst attractive shrubs and landscaping. The American College in Bryn Mawr, Pennsylvania, is such a place, with handsome buildings designed by some of Philadelphia's best architects, and the grounds and planting, extremely well-kept, are the pride of all associated with the institution.

The Wang Institute of Graduate Studies, too, has a lovely 200-acre site in the rural Massachusetts' countryside along the Merrimac River. Here, a large, substantial building made of granite quarried from the property dominates the setting and overlooks a charming small pond and picnic area. Good hiking trails lead off into the surrounding woods. The main building, which was formerly used by the Marist Brothers' order as a seminary for boys, has been thoroughly renovated; classrooms, a model high-tech seminar room, and shiny, efficient computers replace the Brothers' cells. Self-sufficient equipment has replaced the self-sufficient community that had farm animals, gardens, carpentry shops, and canning factory. The little buildings remain as reminders of the past.

In an urban setting, but with unmistakable campus atmosphere, complete with intramural sports, fraternities and sororities, GMI Engineering and Management Institute has its academic building, campus center, and residence hall located on 45 acres in Flint, Michigan. Some 2,300 undergraduates are studying for their bachelor's degree in electrical, industrial, or mechanical engineering or industrial management. The new master's program emanates from this campus.

Northrop University in Inglewood, California, is also in urban surroundings and not far from the Los Angeles International Airport. The

99

Central, West, and North campuses, separated by a few city blocks, contain the various engineering, technology, business, and law schools together with the student union building, residence hall, and Alumni Library. Its physical arrangement is like a small New York University or Columbia.

Other corporate colleges or institutes, housed in wings or sections of larger buildings, look more like graduate departments in universities. The Rand Graduate Institute is so located in part of the Corporation's headquarters in Santa Monica. Similarly, the Arthur D. Little Management Education Institute occupies a wing in one of the connected buildings that comprise the Cambridge, Massachusetts center of corporate activities. In both instances, classrooms, the library and computer center, and offices are functionally clustered. One feels the closer relationship to the parent corporation in the physical setting and, in both cases, the faculty come mainly from the corporation. Each, however, operates as an independent entity, separate from its founding corporate father, in determining its curriculum and standards.

Like a graduate school in its separate building on a university campus, the Institute of Health Professions occupies its own house, converted for educational use, directly across the street from the main complex of the Massachusetts General Hospital Corporation, which is its sponsor and also provides the clinical and laboratory facilities for Institute students.

A few short blocks away, in downtown Boston, the American Institute of Banking has its classrooms and offices on a spacious floor in a well-designed, modern, commercial complex. At the same time, the Institute manages educational programs in 12 other locations around the city, which the director hopes to consolidate into three major centers. In this case, the physical setting and branches are more like a community college, and the employed students are working, almost all part time, for the associate degree of business administration in banking studies.

Comparing the corporate institutions' physical settings to customary models of traditional educational establishments, however, overlooks those that have nontraditional delivery systems that can operate actually from any place. GMI's videotaped courses for their first master's degree in manufacturing management are a case in point. Courses are delivered to the plant or industry where the engineers are working; classrooms are

100

on site. Small groups assemble with a local coordinator in charge of support services and materials. Some 150 persons are studying in ten different locations in four states.

This delivery system has proven to be effective and efficient, particularly in engineering education. Engineers seem to be light-years ahead of other professions in using media for education and updating. Universities co-operating in programs of this type (Association for Media-Based Continuing Education for Engineers) were instrumental in starting the new National Technological University.

Another nontraditional pattern that takes courses to the students is the American College's plan of national coursework, prepared and distributed from the central campus in Bryn Mawr, Pennsylvania. A novel aspect of this program is the new "Examinations on Demand" available through the PLATO computerized system at Control Data Learning Centers in metropolitan areas throughout the United States.

One more example of a corporate program that is easily movable and completely tailored for the individual student is the Master of Management degree based on behavioral competency and offered by the American Management Associations' Institute. Each candidate undergoes an initial audit of his or her managerial abilities and skills, and a personal learning plan is prepared accordingly that may include study at a traditional school, seminars at AMA, performance evaluation on the job and so forth. Alternatives provide the person with choice and flexibility in satisfying requirements. The program, already authorized in California, is awaiting approval in New York State.

FOUR CORPORATE COLLEGES: A CLOSER LOOK

To illustrate not only the wide range of differences in development, curriculum, and purposes, but also to indicate the characteristics shared by many, four institutions are described in individual detail. The American College is an example of evolution to degree-granting status and nontraditional teaching systems; the Wang Institute of Graduate Studies and the Rand Graduate Institute are relatively new institutions at high levels of academic work; and The American Institute of Banking at Boston represents work given for the Associate Degree. In each case, the question was asked: Why start degree programs?

THE AMERICAN COLLEGE: This college, one of the two oldest in the group (along with General Motors Institute) started in 1927 as The American College of Life Underwriters and for most of its existence was known to the public for its Chartered Life Underwriter (CLU) professional designation and diploma. In 1976, the name was legally shortened when the college was reincorporated in the Commonwealth of Pennsylvania as a degree-granting institution with authority to give the Master of Science in Financial Services. In 1982 it was so authorized to also grant the Master of Science in Management.

Over the years, the curricular offerings had steadily broadened, and the more restrictive name was no longer considered appropriate. In addition to the earlier program for insurance professionals (CLU), the college gives the Chartered Financial Consultant diploma and designation, and a variety of short intensive courses as part of the advanced work in its Graduate School.

Reflecting changes in the economic world, the student body now includes a wide spectrum of career professionals from accounting, trust banking, investments, pension and estate planning, and attorneys, as well as persons from insurance companies. Financial services are multiplying rapidly in our society and judged to be one of the major growth areas. The college is obviously serving a need that is not being met in other established educational institutions for significant numbers of people.

Enrollments in the several programs attest to the great demand that exists for further professional education. In the oldest diploma program, the CLU, some 50,000 men and women are participating, and 2,500 annually receive diplomas. On average, it takes four to five years to complete the work, and about one-half of those starting the first year drop out. Recently, the number of women students has increased noticeably and they comprise nearly one-fourth of new matriculants. In the Chartered Financial Consultant program, begun in 1982, nearly 3,000 have already earned the certificate.

The academic background of students is rising, and now the great

102

majority are college graduates. They are studying part time while employed, and almost all their course work is subsidized by employers.

Ten courses are required for the CLU, each considered the equivalent of three semester hours. It is an exacting program: course materials—study guides, text, cassette reviews, and audiovisual aids—are prepared on the central campus by 40 full-time resident faculty and constantly evaluated and updated. More than 50 percent of the faculty have Ph.D. or Doctor of Jurisprudence degrees.

Classrooms are all over the country in more than 250 locations. Students may join formal classrooms, meet informally with peers, or study independently. In the last ten years—with the increasing quality of study guides—organized classes have lost ground to informal groups and independent study. The college catalog makes clear that it is not a correspondence course; instead, it is an "open university" with national coursework and carefully controlled examinations that are administered in cooperation with 300 colleges and universities.

If the student prefers and feels adequately prepared, he or she can opt for the exam on demand, go into a Control Data Corporation center, and take it. Programmed with 400 questions developed by the college's Examination Faculty and consultants, the computer selects 100 covering appropriate materials—each time a different test—and the student sees the pass or fail immediately upon completion. Pass merits the congratulations, stars, and sparklers for which the PLATO system has become famous. It takes only a week longer for the student to receive an analysis of his answers, which is still better than the four to six weeks he waits for examination results in the ordinary mode at the college. The new method is gaining enthusiastic reception.

The American College is looking to the future, experimenting, and testing new technologies and delivery systems. In software, their research staff has developed "Money Manager," a program that can be used on Apple, IBM, or Wang computers. It is not a course for credit, but a tool guiding the manager in dealing with clients, after he has taken the course on Advanced Estate Planning. Approximately 2,000 professionals have purchased it since 1982.

Although no formal courses have yet appeared as software, a video-conference was held in the spring, 1984, for 2,000 financial planners to discuss further possibilities. From 80 locations, via satellite, the one-day session concentrated on computer hardware and software for use in financial planning. Participants also discussed the teleconferencing technique for instruction in certain types of content amenable to it.

Against this backdrop, two Master of Science degree programs were inaugurated: the M.S. in Financial Services and the M.S. in Management. Fifteen hundred are enrolled in the former, which has 450 graduates, and 500 are studying thus far in the latter. Technology has not invaded the graduate level, which remains more traditional except that national course work forms the basis for the 36 credits required. A two-week residency on the main campus is obligatory with two final seminars. The examinations are in essay style, so the PLATO system is out.

Study is limited to seven years for either master's degree; faculty are regularly available for student advising; and again, the course materials are impressive in content, clarity, and design for learning. Organized in 15 assignments, each course includes a study guide, extensive readings selected by the faculty, a text or two from the field, and copies of state and federal regulations when needed. The several volumes constitute a heavy package with more than ample materials for the candidate.

Why did the American College decide to offer the Master of Science in Management (MSM) degree, and how does it differ from the usual MBA program? Answers are prompt and unambivalent. The college dean explains that, compared to the usual MBA, their program is more behavioral oriented, more geared to leadership and management of professionals (not blue collar workers); case studies are selected for service industries rather than manufacturing which MBA studies reflect. The MSM does not emphasize quantitative analysis, and is not based on core requirements of marketing, economics and finance. It is assumed that the candidate who has experience is already familiar with these aspects of the business world.

Comparably, the Master of Science in Financial Services is unique and differs from the conventional MBA since its focus is not on managing a business enterprise. Instead, focus is placed on analyzing, planning, im-

104

plementing, and coordinating complex financial programs—especially for individuals, families, and corporate administrators.

The college decided to add the graduate degree programs because of a perceived need—the same reason the American College started in the first place. And it is the same reason why other corporate colleges started, some in response to internal needs of a company, others to serve wider needs in industry and society.

More specifically, the American College was founded with strong support from the National Association for Life Underwriters to upgrade the profession and set standards for performance. National scandals in the insurance business had led to legislation for control, but business leaders felt education could best provide the understanding and ethical standards needed in sales practices. This early goal has not been lost. In both masters' programs, one of the final seminars required on campus is "Human Relations and Ethics." Furthermore, the degree can be withheld upon a character and professional conduct check.

In the early years of trying to start the college, many attempts were made to get the cooperation of universities, but, generally, academicians were uninterested or looked down on the field of insurance. Shortsightedly, they questioned: Where were the textbooks and what was to be taught?

Thus the American College began in the attic of a walk-up building, outgrew the next headquarters in a fine old house near the University of Pennsylvania, and moved on to its present 40-acre campus with seven buildings, including the Graduate Center with a 50-room residence wing. As an institution, the college is accredited by the Commission on Higher Education of the Middle States Association of Colleges and Schools.

WANG INSTITUTE OF GRADUATE STUDIES: A very different sort of place, the Wang Institute of Graduate Studies nevertheless shares certain key characteristics with the American College and other corporate educational institutes. Although it began with strong personal initiative and financial support from Dr. An Wang (with additional support from Wang Laboratories, Inc.) the institute, too, was to serve the whole industry by providing more highly skilled software engineers and specialists. And it, too, was to help establish high standards for the new profession. The program emphasizes the importance of professional practices and ethics.

It is no secret that the field of software development—the content to accompany computer hardware—is in disarray. As a new field without experience or age, software is frequently produced by chance or intuition, on an ad hoc basis, or for quick monetary returns. Literally thousands of independent, uninstructed operators are playing around with programs and attempting fast sales, often at the cost of the American consumer. Like the insurance business at the turn of the century, the new software field needs to be regularized and to develop professionalism. It requires formalization in process, procedures that are transferable to the development of other programs, and standards for quality.

And again, as in the case of the American College or other corporate institutes, universities either did not, or could not, provide the needed programs. For three years, Harvard had tried a similar program that failed due to conflicts between traditional academic requirements and the multidisciplinary studies essential to the new field. Once more, theory could not accommodate reality and practice.[4]

For these reasons and, perhaps foremost, because no other place was offering the needed educational program, the Wang Institute came into being. With a charter granted in 1979 by the Commonwealth of Massachusetts, authorization was given to grant the Master of Software Engineering (MSE) degree. Since then, accreditation candidacy status has been awarded by the New England Association of Schools and Colleges.

Early in the development of the institute, other companies and business leaders joined in support and became founding sponsors. Besides money and equipment, 15 companies sponsored students during the 1981-82 school year and continue to do so on tuition refund plans. Hewlett-Packard was first to give a full scholarship (plus 75 percent of salary) for an employee to attend. Others participating are Digital Equipment, Data General, Apple, Prime Computer, Raytheon, Honeywell, and so on. Some of them are now part of an established Corporate Associate Program.

Thus, the Wang Institute is obviously not—and never was—an institution serving only the Wang Labs. It is an independent, nonprofit institution operating on a budget of about $1.5 million. Dr. Wang personally

106

has guaranteed the institute's future by a set of trusts to build endowment over the next decade.

Enrollment at Wang is about 35 students, mostly part time, and great expansion in numbers is not anticipated. Instead, the goal is to train an elite cadre for the field. Perhaps in five years, there may be 100 students in the master's program under the School of Information Technology, the first school created by the institute.

A second program of a quite different type has recently been introduced to support research in the humanities and social sciences. It is a post-doctoral Fellowship Program in Chinese Studies that is administered by the Graduate Institute, but the scholars' research is done at other institutions.

Other new developments closer to the School of Information Technology may include further work in the computer sciences, and possibly a coordinated undergraduate-graduate program with another institution. Three years' undergraduate work could be combined with two years at the Wang Institute for a graduate degree. Another idea under investigation is the doctorate in software engineering, which might be modelled on medical doctoral education, emphasizing the practice (clinical) aspects. Still another possibility is a master's degree in systems engineering (hardware). Decisions will be made on the basis of marketplace needs. Such new programs are viewed as evolutionary from the present specialized MSE degree.

Above all, the faculty and others vital to the Institute of Graduate Studies see it as of university caliber and point out, for example, that products developed by student teams—an essential part of the curriculum—will go into the public domain as would be the case in "all other universities." A faculty committee constitutes the Products Release Board and judges whether a project is worthy of distribution. If it is favorably decided, anyone can get the documentation and tape for a small fee that covers reproduction cost, or free if a tape is provided with the request. Such products are a new venture, and possibly regular charges will be set in the future. Still, the copyright is held by the institute, as it would be held by a university press for the publication of a thesis.

Wang's admissions standards are comparable to, if not more rigorous than, some of the best graduate schools. They assure extremely able and bright students. In addition to the bachelor's degree with a minimum average of B, transcripts, and the GRE General Aptitude Test (within the last three years), candidates must have a year's professional experience in a software related field, three letters of recommendation from professionals, and expertise in specific areas of mathematics and computer science that are spelled out in detail. They must also demonstrate written communication skills by submitting a short essay on a technical subject. Highly selective admissions, of course, reduce attrition and guarantee strongly motivated students who "expect to work seventy hours a week."

Course work at Wang is as demanding for students as it is for faculty who must constantly refresh their knowledge to remain *au courant* with new developments appearing in this field. Faculty bear heavy teaching loads, integrate their courses with the teaching of others, and operate on a contract basis (no tenure). Salaries are competitive with business, and working hours are longer.

A National Academic Advisory Committee, set up early in discussions that led to the institute's establishment, is comprised of experts from Harvard, Princeton, the University of Michigan, and Digital Equipment, Apollo, Wang Labs, and Bell Telephone Laboratories. They play an active part in evaluating the courses being given and in considering curricular changes and decisions for new degree programs. Excitement and high energy levels pervade the atmosphere at the institute. Maybe it is the innovative nature of the place, its youth, and freedom to experiment, its unique nature. Whatever the cause, there is a confident view toward expanded educational horizons for the Wang Institute of Graduate Studies.

RAND GRADUATE INSTITUTE: The Rand Ph.D. is another example of high level academic work given by a corporation but, in this case, it is an integral part of the parent company although autonomous in setting its standards and curricular program. Founded in 1970, the Rand Graduate Institute began its innovative program in policy analysis that combines formal academic courses and seminar workshops with on-the-job training in Rand research projects on real issues of public policy concerning domestic, international, and national security problems. The Institute "seeks to advance the methods and tools of policy research, as well as the academic disciplines it uses."

Asked why they decided to set up their own graduate program, Dean Charles Wolf, Jr., replied in his usual organized fashion. Their planning committee considered *whether* Rand should do something more in education and, if so, *why* and *what*. Their thinking and answers are summarized:

Whether. Rand already had (and still has) summer interns from whom they select a few to employ. Some 30-40 Rand staff were teaching elsewhere, and there was further interaction through consultants and exchanges with other educational institutions. So why was more needed?

Why. The National Science Foundation had asserted the need for interdisciplinary studies—including scientific fields—on national problems. More was needed than the usual interdisciplinary work in social sciences. The public service factor was not only apparent but essential.

Further, Rand had a corporate interest and saw it as good for the image of the company and as an aid to recruitment and retention of staff. (Smart people often want interaction—teaching—with bright, younger minds.) Around 1970, Vietnam troubles and antimilitary attitudes had caused some Rand staff to leave for universities. Moreover, it was a challenge, an exciting venture. It would be fun to start a new institute and design the program.

What. They first considered cooperation with the California Institute of Technology or the University of California at Los Angeles. Too many complications. Would courses be given at the university and the dissertation at Rand? How would funding be handled? Who would award the degree? And so on and on. "Collaborative logistics were so formidable that they feared curriculum and substance would get short-changed."

Therefore, Rand would do it alone. Its resources in expertise, ideas, experience, and knowledge are outstanding. From the 500 professional staff at Rand, there are some 175 Ph.D.'s to be drawn upon as faculty. There is a list of those waiting to be invited. A Committee on Curriculum and Appointments approves faculty who are part time, generally teaching one trimester or ten-week course a year. Retaining full salary, they receive an additional amount from the institute on a scale related to the University of California rate of pay. To remain on the faculty, one teaches at least once in three years.

In addition to the institute's internal committees on curriculum, admissions, and review of students' work, there is a larger Rand Advisory Board of faculty, other senior research staff and students, and another committee of Rand trustees to oversee the institute. For more links with the outside educational community, an Academic Advisory Board of distinguished scholars from major universities meets twice a year to review the program and advise.

The program exploits the research environment and, in turn, contributes to it. A broad spectrum of disciplinary studies are systematically related to the policy analysis of multidisciplinary problems. Structurally, the curriculum comprises three categories of analytical core courses covering concepts, theory, tools, and techniques central to policy analysis; seminar workshops based on completed Rand studies; and on-the-job training in ongoing Rand policy research projects leading to a doctoral dissertation.

In a description of its educational pattern, the analogy is drawn between the institute's core courses and medical school lectures, its workshops to medicine's rotating internships, and its on-the-job training to medicine's residencies. But a major and important difference is emphasized: whereas medicine offers theory and training *serially*, the institute offers them *simultaneously*. A primary objective of the institute is the integration of formal learning with application. Arguing with the educational system based on the discipline and then its application, the institute points out that, particularly at advanced levels, single disciplines are inadequate in confronting policy problems of society that are inevitably multidisciplinary. Hence, application is embedded within a broad curriculum.

One may ask how broad the curriculum is, and especially how broad a choice there is for dissertation topics based on current Rand projects. Students come with backgrounds particularly in physical or biological sciences, social sciences and mathematics. Building on these fields, institute work covers micro- and macroeconomics, organization theory and behavior, game theory and application, psychological and political aspects of policy making, and social implications (more than values and ethics),

110

especially in such workshop topics as criminal justice, education, housing, and regulatory policy. Technology, computer science, statistics, and various techniques of analysis are offered, as well as the uses of history in providing data for policy research.

And, contrary to what may be the general public's understanding, the Rand Corporation has considerable spread in its contracts. While it used to be 90 percent on international and national security issues, the proportion a few years ago was about equal between those issues and domestic concerns. Currently, the proportion runs around 62 percent international and national security with 38 percent domestic. So there is much better balance available for choice than one might expect, and student dissertation topics reflect the breadth. Topics range from the expected technical aspects and analysis of air force and defense subjects to the quality of health care for certain infectious diseases in a disadvantaged population, "The Role of the School Principal in Implementing Alternatives," "Countering Terrorism in Israel," and "The Effect of Economic Interdependence on Foreign Policy Cooperation." Interestingly, it appears that foreign students may tend to select the topics of broader social concern.

The 60 graduate fellows enrolled at Rand come from a variety of institutions and foreign countries, with perhaps one-third from Stanford and Ivy League schools. Entrance requirements are stiff and comparable to those of the Wang Institute, but with the Master's degree or equivalent already in hand. It is a most intellectually demanding and stringently scheduled course: full-time students taking three courses per trimester, 18 for graduation plus the dissertation. Of 68 fellows who passed written and oral examinations between 1973 and 1983, 27 had received the doctorate by 1983, and five or six other dissertations were in an advanced stage. Four or five graduate each year.

There is, however, an enlightened feature that counters the high cost in time, energy and tuition ($6,500 in 1983-84). When the candidate starts on-the-job training for half-time during the academic year and full-time in summer, he or she is paid a median salary of $15,000-18,000 depending on experience and the area of work. Moreover, this is non-taxable since it is an integral part of the education. It is a costly program

111

supported in roughly equal parts by tuition, the Rand Corporation and grants from foundations like Sloan and Ford.

Again, like the Wang Institute and other corporate programs, admissions are open to those qualified, and graduates go on to many different positions. It is not a training ground for the Rand Corporation, which employs directly very few, believing it is best for the graduates to gain experience elsewhere. So they go mainly to the federal government, increasingly to state and local agencies in such positions as legislative analysts, and into the private sector, usually where it interfaces with public policies in industries like oil, utilities and others.

Great expansion of the institute's Ph.D. program is not envisaged, but two study fields of special importance have lately been added and, interestingly, in conjunction with the University of California at Los Angeles. Having eschewed cooperative ventures when the institute was founded, the leadership has now devised a scheme that holds promise in providing the expertise needed for the fields and in offering considerable choice for the fortunate graduate fellows.

The two institutions have established cooperative programs in the Rand/UCLA Centers for Health Policy Study, and for Study of Soviet International Behavior. The centers award fellowships—up to five in each—and a certain number of courses are taken in each program under the aegis of the centers. Aside from this, however, the programs are separate. Students are admitted to one institution or the other and receive its doctorate according to requirements.

In Health Policy Study, cross registration is permitted for a limited number of courses approved by the center and the institution granting credit. Ongoing research projects at each institution provide dissertation topics and experience for the fellow. The Schools of Public Health and Medicine are the cooperating units from UCLA and on the other side, the Rand Graduate Institute and Rand's own Health Sciences Program. Fellows are supported generously by the Pew Memorial Trust.

The Center for the Study of Soviet International Behavior operates comparably with UCLA's departments of economics, history, and political science cooperating with the Rand Graduate Institute that gives its doctorate in policy analysis. Together they have more than 20 faculty

112

and research staff members specializing in pertinent areas. It is a significant concentration of expertise with Rand's capabilities in Soviet foreign and military policy and the broad infrastructure in Russian and East European graduate training at the university. Fellowships are financed by the center and the Rand Corporation, through a grant from the Rockefeller Foundation.

Other new activities seen by the institute as "glimmers," or ideas for further thought are mid-career education for executives of the large *Fortune* 500 companies that might be six-week summer programs given as mini-versions of parts of the curriculum, and external, foreign workshops on a limited scale, such as the institute's recent seminar staged in China for the Academy for Social Sciences.

The Rand Graduate Institute presents a relatively rare opportunity in this country on the Ph.D. level; just three other comparable schools of public policy exist—at Berkeley, Harvard and Carnegie Mellon where it is the School of Urban and Public Affairs. Other programs are on the master's level. Yet, the complexities of planning and determining public policies present one of the greatest challenges of our time. More research universities could well take up the challenge of relating various fields of study with new tools and techniques of analysis to the multidisciplinary problems confronting all societies.

AMERICAN INSTITUTE OF BANKING AT BOSTON: The American Institute of Banking (AIB) is a nationwide organization serving as the primary educational arm of the American Bankers Association. Regional "chapters" around the country provide training and education for banking personnel in the particular geographic area. Curiously, banking is one of the very few industries in the United States that is organized nationally for its educational programs.

Boston's chapter, though not the biggest in numbers, is one of the oldest and is the first to award an academic degree, the Associate Degree of Business Administration in Banking Studies. Authorized by the Massachusetts Board of Regents in 1979, the institute has candidacy status voted by the New England Association of Schools and Colleges and expects full status in 1985. Such academic authority was sought because of "an increasing desire for educational recognition by the banking community."

Midst the general comings and goings of nearly 9,000 persons annually taking various courses and special programs at the institute, the degree program has 140 formally enrolled in a well-conceived and tightly structured curriculum. All 63 semester hours are required courses with the exception of one elective in each of three possible major concentrations. The student basically makes one important decision: the choice of the major banking concentration that will constitute one-third of the degree work. The choice is made from a fairly wide field: bank auditing, branch administration, credit and loan, savings bank management; systems, data processing, and operations; and trust education.

Arts and sciences and general business courses each take another one-third, thus making the total necessary for graduation. Class attendance is required, as is an overall grade point average of C. Students must take at least one course during the fall and spring semesters and complete a minimum of nine semester hours each calendar year. There is no "dropping in or out" for course work. All work for the degree must be completed within ten years of the initial registration date.

Courses are in evening hours and Saturday mornings, usually meeting once a week for two and one-half hours. Summer session is more intensive with classes scheduled twice weekly. All students are part time while they work full time in the banks sponsoring them and paying their tuition. Officially, students from the general public can enroll and pay their own way, but this is most infrequent.

Not wishing to set up academic departments and yet realizing the need for cohesion among faculty—particularly since all are part time—the institute created nine different study areas, such as liberal arts or accounting and finance, each with a chairman. Faculty in each group exchange notes on their classroom approach and how they are teaching the same or similar courses.

Moreover, faculty are accustomed to continuing evaluation from their students, and class visitation by peers and the administrators. It is a formal evaluation process. For example, if an administrator is doing it, no notes are made in the class, but they are recorded immediately afterward according to a prepared outline of points for observation. Within 24 hours, the observer orally discusses the points with the faculty member. As an ongoing and expected practice, understood to be for the improvement of teaching, evaluations have not been divisive or seen as threatening.

Ninety percent of the 200 faculty members come from the banking profession and the others, teaching U.S. History, English and so on, are from other educational institutions like Suffolk and Northeastern Universities with whom, incidentally, the institute maintains a cooperative transfer of credit for certain degree work at the universities.

The AIB at Boston issues each semester a *Handbook of Course Descriptions* that challenges the typical college vagueness in course listings. In clear, concise English, each course is succinctly presented with its purpose, the results a student *can* expect to achieve, and a list of detailed items that the course examines. Compared to many community colleges, which AIB sees as its main competitors, the institute is highly organized and runs a no-nonsense, ship-shape program. It runs like a business, which it is—in banking education. And its motto claims "The Competitive Edge."

AIB's motto suggests another theme well publicized at Hamburger University: "Training is the Key." McDonald's Management Institute, as part of the university, marks its entry into direct degree work with a program for the Associate of Applied Science in Business Management. Before, the university concentrated on its advanced operations courses, given in two-week seminars for 2,000 employees a year. The campus is also the preparation center for extensive in-house training materials that are used in local restaurants for *all* employees in every type of work. McDonald's has by far the most thorough and extensive training program of any corporation examined. Every single employee is actually required to meet training and performance standards. The corporation truly believes its motto.

Because employees cannot attend classes for long periods of time on the central campus, the degree courses are to be taken on a part-time, correspondence basis. Transfer credits will be accepted, particularly for the 15 hours required in general liberal arts courses. To enroll, the employee must be at least in middle management or a supervisory position.

GENERAL CHARACTERISTICS

Regardless of the unique aspects of each corporate institute or college, some general characteristics are notable. First, almost all of these colleges are nonprofit, and most are private, independent institutions, comparable in this respect to traditional private colleges. Four are integral or organized as part of their parent corporation, which itself is nonprofit. This is the case with Rand's Graduate Institute, the Massachusetts General Hospital's Institute of Health Professions, and the two management institutes of the American Management Associations and the Midwest Industrial Management Association. Hamburger University's Institute is integral to the McDonald Corporation as is Arthur D. Little's Institute but, in both instances, although the education program is subsidized by the profit-making corporation, it does not operate with profit.

Only two—the DeVry Institutes, which are a subsidiary of Bell and Howell, and Watterson College owned by Jostens, Inc., are organized as proprietary, for profit or, as some prefer to say, tax-paying schools. Both institutions, however, are completely approved by the educational accrediting associations in their regions: the North Central for DeVry, and the Southern Association of Colleges and Schools for Watterson College.

In addition, DeVry is accredited by the two major professional accreditation bodies for engineering and technology and for trade and technical schools. Watterson is also accredited by the Association of Independent Colleges and Schools, which is recognized by the U.S. Department of Education as the accreditor for business schools. So credentials are all in order and in full display for both. This also means, of course, that their students are eligible for federal and state financial aid and loan programs, regardless of their profit-making status.

It would be short-sighted to think that proprietary status per se has any direct bearing on the quality of academic work given. Such charges may be unfortunately true in some cases, but in others they are distinctly false. Work in electronics engineering, for example, at DeVry Institutes is of a high academic order and widely recognized as superior.

In the current economic environment with pressures toward career education, Bell and Howell makes a handsome profit from the DeVry

116

Institutes, which had tuition revenues of $117 million in 1983 and earned $16.8 million. The student body has expanded to over 30,000 from 7,000 in 1977, and facilities and campuses are rapidly expanding to keep up. With 11 institutes in the United States and Canada, another new campus is scheduled for next year.

At DeVry, the profit is achieved by operational efficiencies and by stated limits in programs offered. Facilities are used 12 months a year with two shifts a day; professors are paid solely to teach, not to write or publish, and there is virtually none of the campus life or student activities that traditional colleges offer. As Donald N. Frey, Bell and Howell's chairman and chief executive, said of DeVry schools, "We don't have a glee club or student union; there is no marching band or cheerleaders. These are overhead costs, and they're expensive."[5] DeVry actively supports its graduates, and their placement record is enviable.

With the profits shown, no wonder a takeover was attempted by the National Education Corporation, which already owns 47 technical schools, and was fiercely resisted by Bell and Howell. As a result, "DeVRY, Inc." was created, with the Bell and Howell Company retaining 85 percent of the stock. DeVry Institutes have spawned other private, profit-making schools like the Keller Graduate School of Management that was started in 1973 by two men who left the Bell and Howell Education Group. Six hundred students have since graduated with the MBA degree.

Although the educational establishment has seldom seen it, there is money to be made in education and training, and it can be done with quality programs. In early 1984, the Grumman Corporation purchased the Center for Computer Education in West Newton, Massachusetts. The Center's president, boasting that it was "the Amherst of business schools," welcomed the new sponsorship of the large international corporation and assured students and public alike that only the name was changing to Grumman Data Systems Institute. When asked whether an academic degree was contemplated, the answer was that there was talk about it, no action yet, but hope that it might become degree granting. Undoubtedly the more than 100 students—most with college degrees—will add pressure to go beyond the diploma and grant an advanced degree. The Grumman

Institute is the first to offer each student a guaranteed internship with a high-tech firm.[6]

Making a business of schools is emerging as a growth industry. Fred Hechinger reports that several big companies—International Telephone and Telegraph and the Encyclopedia Britannica Educational Corporation along with Bell and Howell—are considering plans for proprietary elementary and secondary schools, believing it may be "a sound investment and a public service." The idea raises questions as well as fears, but it could also challenge "present monopolistic, status quo-bound practices" in the public school system.[7]

A study of proprietary schools and trends is long overdue, but the two for-profit networks of DeVry Institutes and Watterson College in this analysis appear academically sound as well as financially successful. Still, the majority of corporate institutes and colleges being considered here remain nonprofit.

Second, the academic degrees being given by corporate colleges range from the associate to the doctorate. Contrary to a generally held assumption, the associate level is not the most prevalent. Instead, eleven institutions offer the master's degree, seven the associate, five have bachelor's level programs, and three confer the Ph.D. or J.D. Several institutions offer work at various levels.

Third, the credentials of these colleges and institutes are solid. All are authorized in their own states except the AMA's Institute of Management Competency which has degree authority in California but awaits a decision in New York State. Almost all are accredited or have candidacy status or applications in process (the newer ones) with the regional higher education associations that evaluate traditional colleges and universities. Two—AMA's and Hamburger University's institutes—that are in the formation stage are planning to apply at the appropriate time. Many are additionally recognized by various technical and professional associations. On the basis of accreditation processes in the United States, these institutions are generally full-fledged members of the approved higher education community.

Fourth, almost all of the corporate institutions have governance, structure, and academic and administrative titles that parallel traditional colleges and universities. The familiar academic hierarchy of presidents,

118

provosts and deans, admissions and faculty curriculum committees prevails generally even in the more innovative institutes. College catalogs explain requirements for graduation and admission, transfer credits, life on the campus, residential arrangements, and costs. Faculty lists with qualifications and sometimes recent publications accompany course descriptions. It is the customary world of academe with boards of trustees or directors and, in the older institutions, active alumni associations contributing to financial support.

One could assume that when a business corporation decides to start an educational institute or college, the academic model floats into view and becomes the guiding vision for the institute's formation—its structure and organization. To some extent this may occur, but a more dominant factor is also at work: the academic accreditation process itself. Accreditation is a standardizing force that carries conformity and asks adherence to established practices as evidence of standards and quality.[8] And so we find academic terminology, hierarchy, and trappings on most of the accredited corporate campuses, and yet the institutions may be quite innovative and different from academe in other ways.

There is, for example, a far greater use of part-time faculty in the corporate institution, a practice often frowned upon in traditional higher education and often by accrediting commissions. Still it is a deliberate and defended policy at corporate colleges. They engage experts part time who continue active research or other employment in the company pertinent to their teaching. Work experience is a major requirement for faculty in most corporate education. As the dean at Hamburger University put it, "We take the experienced men in operations and management, and then teach them to teach. We do not take educators."

Further, even when faculty are full-time, as at several of the institutes, there is no tenure policy. Instead, it is a contractual basis with hours and salaries more comparable to the corporate business world.

Another difference from traditional colleges is the noticeable absence of academic departments and the notable prevalence of multidisciplinary studies. Faculty members at Massachusetts General Hospital's Institute of Health Professions, for example, must express their willingness to use multidisciplinary approaches and cooperate with disciplines other than

119

their own before they are employed. There are no departments at the American Institute of Banking at Boston; Rand Graduate Institute saw the importance of interdisciplinary studies including the sciences as an important reason for starting their program in policy analysis; Wang's Institute, too, needed the broader academic approach. The American Graduate School of International Management has a tripartite curriculum in which each area is multidisciplinary in itself. World business covers functional specialties in finance and business, advanced managerial and marketing techniques; international studies includes current economic, social, political and cultural aspects in one or more areas of the world required for study; and modern languages offer an intensive and functional command in any of eight tongues including Arabic, Mandarin Chinese, and Brazilian Portuguese, after which courses are given solely in the foreign language on such subjects as procedures and regulations relevant to international managers in a particular region of the world. Many other corporate institutes have been created to cross subject matter lines for functional purposes: to solve problems and operate more effectively.

As a result of broader academic studies and less narrow departmentalism, as well as no tenure policy, these institutes possess a flexibility and freedom to adjust curricula or requirements. Even the older institutions of the group, like GMI or the American College, have retained an ability to change and adjust fairly quickly compared to colleges built around major subject matter requirements in many often small and separate departments.

One other characteristic stands out clearly in corporate classrooms: an emphasis upon continuing evaluation of faculty and courses. Several colleges have advisory boards of scholars and experts from other institutions and companies that frequently review curricula and individual course outlines. Internal course evaluations of teaching and materials by students, colleagues and administrators are also routinized and taken for granted. Compared to traditional colleges, there seems to be less fear of criticism and more openness toward analysis for improvement on the part of the teacher. Since performance evaluation is an accepted part of the business world, it is not surprising to find it as part of the education world being created by business corporations.

Several of the corporate institutions now granting their own degrees tried at the beginning to cooperate with established colleges and universities. This was true at Rand, the American College, and the Wang Institute. It was also the case at Arthur D. Little's Management Education Institute which, in its earliest days, had Syracuse University faculty teaching business fundamentals and Tufts faculty from the Fletcher School teaching international trade courses. These arrangements were less than successful for both the faculty and the first students, Nigerians, who expected to learn how to manage industrial development projects in Africa.[9]

More than culture shock and transition for both students and faculty, the mismatch was basically between the theoretical and general materials, and the practical agridevelopment and quantitative fundamentals needed to initiate and manage programs in Nigeria. It was soon evident that Arthur D. Little's staff could fill this bill better than university professors.

It is the age-old problem of the integration of theory and practice, of the application of knowledge and training in what is repeatedly called "the real world"—the combination of conceptual study and actual work. The attempt to make learning useful is probably the foremost attribute of all the corporate colleges, whether in associate level or Ph.D. programs.

Their programs are largely technical and professional in nature; degrees are in the sciences, in many specialized types of engineering, in computer sciences, in health areas, and in business areas and management. The newer ones, particularly, focus on masters' degrees in management and point out their differences with the older, institutionalized MBA programs in business schools.

Corporate college catalogs state their goals with refreshing clarity; usually it is an unambiguous statement of objectives that is quite specific and explains what the student may expect to achieve in skills, competency, and behavior, as well as knowledge.

Always, they have started in response to a perceived need: a market gap, a vacuum unfilled by traditional higher education. And although the corporate or business group has often invited the assistance of colleges

121

and universities, cooperative efforts in these cases do not have a high success record—particularly when the "perceived need" involves a new field or extension of the application of knowledge.

Established higher education institutions historically have been slow to introduce new fields; they have doubted their "academic" merit, they have waited for emerging disciplines to prove their intellectual respectability. It took a long time before the laboratory sciences were recognized on university property. Law and medicine grew up outside the ivy-covered walls—under private auspices—and formed powerful professional associations controlling licensing regulations and accreditation processes that still tend to dominate curricula even though law and medicine now have their schools under the university umbrella.

Professional education and setting standards for performance were basic, formative reasons for the establishment of the industrywide institutes and colleges in banking and insurance. These are overriding reasons for the new masters' level work in financial services, in the developing health professions, and in the new field of software engineering.

Since the mid-seventies, degree-granting institutes and colleges—started by noncollegiate bodies—have been appearing with increasing frequency. Corporate groups apparently have concluded that it is easier to go it alone and not bother with cooperative efforts with the traditional establishment. But these newer institutes also reflect the fact that the conditions of education are not static. There is continual growth in new knowledge and new skills for which education and training must be designed and provided. The "perceived needs" are multiplying. The new fields are emerging from laboratories; they are both elemental and incremental as extended applications of knowledge dramatically expand.

What will be the response of traditional higher education to these emerging needs? It is significant that in the last five years or so, the creative laboratories of major research universities and large corporations have moved closer together in research collaboration. This should trigger more university involvement in designing education for the emerging new fields and professions. Thus far, however, the initiative has rested with the business corporations, reflecting industrywide concerns. It is from this private sector—with its financial resources—that the new institutes and colleges are coming.

122

CHAPTER VI

The Learning Business: Emerging Issues

WHILE CORPORATE CLASSROOMS challenge the schools and higher education, a contest is farthest from the corporate mind concerned primarily with productivity and capability—both for workers and customers. Corporations certainly do not intend their training programs to be a threat to established education, which they support in many ways. They simply give education to compensate for what employees lack to perform the task at hand and need for their next responsibilities; they educate to support company research and development, management, and sales. And they have come to see education and training as an investment in human resources. Their programs are large and extensive, and they are seizing upon educational technology to maximize their returns.

Years ago, Lewis Branscomb and Paul Gilmore of IBM perceptively asked:

> If the educational community does not respond to the requirement for continuing education under circumstances that are deemed cost effective by industry, what are the consequences of the further expansion of industrially operated educational institutions, whether represented by classrooms or dispersed computer networks?[1]

And they suggested further that if inhibitions prevented education's use of the developing technologies, "The stage may be set for the emergence of a major profitable learning industry."

The growth of corporate in-house education and especially its curriculum broadening to overlap with colleges, the expansion of corporate colleges and institutes giving their own academic degrees, the National Technological University and other electronic universities, the remarkable development of the private learning industry in the last decade—all give answers to Branscomb's and Gilmore's query. Corporate educational developments are posing an unintended challenge to higher education, and the learning industry is becoming most profitable.

Furthermore, as industry has always had to provide for its particular training needs, it will continue to do so. Corporate projections and the education to support them must be forward looking; they must create the future. The traditional system, in contrast, tends to perpetuate the past, and this is only partially justified by its mission.

Although colleges and universities have as part of their mission the obligation to hand on a cultural heritage and offer some core of knowledge, they are also expected to confront the future through research and scholarly additions to knowledge. Their context is, perforce, larger, and the perspective both wider and more long-ranged than is found usually in corporate classrooms. Expectations of outcome are of a different order in the two systems.

But one wonders whether the distinction will remain very clear in the years ahead. Duplication already blurs the difference. Corporate classrooms must increasingly give courses that deal with the foundations— the fundamentals—of processes involved in production and operations as well as the possibilities inherent in products. Demands of knowledge-intensive industries frequently require the depth and breadth of learning that have been the hallmark of college and university curricula.

At the same time, colleges are increasingly adding courses such as those in computer sciences and business fields that invade corporate curricula. There may be justification for the courses to be given by both systems, their uses differ for students, and diversity continues to be a strength in American education. Some duplication, therefore, may be inevitable and even desirable but, in other instances, duplication becomes wasteful and implies inadequacies in the educational establishment.

IMPLICATIONS FOR EDUCATION

Corporate classrooms should not be so busy teaching the three R's of reading, writing, and arithmetic. Not only is instructional improvement needed in these elementary skills, but basic academic preparation must include mathematics and basic sciences in high schools, and speaking-listening skills. A distressing difference in perception about the need for these abilities appeared between school and business executives in the Center for Public Resources study. Deficiencies can lessen the chance of advancement in the workplace for a lifetime.

Cooperative efforts by schools and local industries seem to be increasing, but often they are focused on vocational training and career development. In many cases, corporate advisers are not involved with basic skills training although they may provide temporary instructors in math and science. Teachers in other subjects seldom encounter them, much less understand the corporate perspective on what high school graduates need to know to get a job and keep it.

Public and private school systems on the secondary level could well investigate the courses being used in corporate classrooms to teach basic communications and computation skills. Methods used there may be more cost effective as well as more effective in learning results and retention. Their goal-oriented training and intensive approach could prove successful with many students.

At the same time, higher education can fill its role more effectively by doing a better job of educating on its own terms. It, too, must ask better performance of students in such basic work as organizing and writing research papers, in oral presentation and clear explanation; corporate trainers should not find it so necessary to teach these abilities, particularly as more college graduates enter the work force. A much better job can be done teaching foreign languages intensively through immersion and follow-up use; corporate classrooms should not need to offer foreign language instruction.

Colleges and universities—without violating their purposes—can give more multidisciplinary consideration to real issues, provide more practical applications of theoretical studies, and add teamwork approaches to teaching and learning methods. Focus exclusively on individual development can lessen a person's ability to contribute cooperatively and work effectively with others.

Similarly, theoretical studies in the absence of actual and possible applications can handicap a good mind, leaving it in speculative limbo. Very

125

often, corporate colleges and institutes are started for multidisciplinary purposes and application of theoretical knowledge. Industry's classrooms reflect these concerns as well as behavioral orientation toward working harmoniously with others and cooperative supervision. Adjustments in higher education along these lines require no deviation from mission.

Many deterents to collaboration stem from matters of style and customary routines. If colleges and universities wish more future cooperation with the corporate classroom, they will have to adjust scheduling and curriculum time frames for more intensive instruction and learn to teach adults more effectively. This can be done by selected professors interested in particular subjects; it hardly requires an across-the-board change in the college structure. Part of the problem in cooperative efforts has been a monolithic attitude, an assumption that the whole institution would be forced to change. Why not, for example, think of individuals who would and could teach on a more intensive basis, juxtaposed with longer blocks of time for research or other activities? Such a schedule would appeal to some faculty.

Nevertheless, experience teaches that collaboration between these two parallel systems is most successful in rather specific areas that are congenial to the needs and capabilities of both, such as engineering, business and management training, and research. As independent R&D labs struggle to stay technologically up to date and search for venture capital that is harder to locate due to increased competition and large start up costs, they are finding linkages with universities may be profitable. Calspan Corporation, an independent lab with aerospace and military intelligence contracts, joined in June, 1984, with the State University of New York at Buffalo to establish a not-for-profit center for biotechnology and life sciences research. Federal funds will be generated that would be virtually closed to Calspan without the university link.[2]

Some universities, following the example of Stanford University's assistance to William Hewlett and David Packard 30 years ago when they were young engineers, are renting space and encouraging entrepreneurs with ideas for high technology. Science Park in New Haven has Yale's cooperation in making available faculty in science and engineering for consultation; and similarly, Princeton is related to the Forrestal Center located there. Rensselaer Polytechnic Institute has its "incubator" for the newly formed small companies and not only offers faculty consultation but students for hire as researchers or programmers, computer and library use, and a director of the project who maintains contacts for possible venture capital.[3]

In such specific instances typical of research, engineering, and business schools, collaboration is desired and usually desirable for both parties. Working closely together in basic and applied research, however, entails more problems for the academic institution, its teaching function related to research, and its fundamental commitment to openness and freedom in its search. Research universities are well aware of the complications inherent in the growing partnerships with corporations. Safeguards are contracted, and the new experiment is underway, no doubt with problems to be encountered as results develop.

Community colleges have an excellent track record in cooperative programs, but again under conditions favorable to their designated mission to serve the community, and their curricula, by design, include more vocational preparation and practical training. Still, the conclusion holds that two-way programs will work best when directly addressed to the needs and abilities on each side of the compact. Therefore, it seems vacuous to issue *general* calls for increased cooperation.

THE LEARNING ENVIRONMENT

Meanwhile new types of bridges are leading to experimental and pervasive collaboration of many types. Microcomputers are linking business and education faster than specific cooperative training programs; the environment has changed. Thousands of entrepreneurial spirits have moved into the marketplace—individuals programming software for all purposes, corporations creating courses to support their computer hardware, and professional associations selling training in a multitude of new forms. Competition is intense. Many are vying for sales in corporate training programs and in education-at-large, the schools and the adult education market. This is the larger environment in which corporate classrooms and school classrooms are functioning, midst a dizzying assortment of teaching aids and prepared courses from which to choose.

The computer courseware field may be crowded, and predictions are

127

for increased growth, but often seen are software designs that flash across the horizon and catch the eye like a meteor only to quickly disappear. Although many experience such brief life spans and thus perhaps slow the explosive growth, courseware production will continue steadily and inevitably because of consumer demand and the recognition by big computer companies that their hardware will sell only with multiple programming uses. It is well known, for example, that when an Apple or an IBM PC hits the market, independent programmers start finding new machine capabilities.

But equally important is the development of multi-system software. "Compatibility" is the name of the game. It increases applications by using electronic architecture to add capability and flexibility to systems. It means creation of single software packages adaptable to many different computers and individual user needs. The wave of the future is to integrate, and thus enhance, computer systems.

The learning industry will be limited only by the imagination and the time it takes to develop the next delivery medium. Currently, voice reproduction—well beyond computer-generated text recitation—is underway. Scott Instruments Corporation has announced an oral teaching machine; it recognizes an individual student's voice answering its question and responds with its own computer-simulated voice. The system teaches spelling, reading, and foreign languages.[4] Digital Equipment has DEC talk, a sophisticated human speech synthesizer using a program developed at MIT, that can be used for two-way communication with a flexible vocabulary on a touchtone phone system.

Many, many other companies, small and large, are in research and experimental stages. Inventors are confident that as computers comprehend the human voice, they will be able to respond to sophisticated and complicated spoken instructions, making them ever more "user friendly" and accessible.

While inventions go on, major hardware companies invest heavily in extending the consumer's choices in software, underwriting in part the courseware market. IBM has entered into joint marketing agreements with Prentice-Hall to offer low-cost software tutorials for the classroom

128

and with Comshare and DunsPlus to provide more courses for microcomputers.

McGraw-Hill is not only adapting its traditional printed words and information data sources for electronic delivery, but it also prepares software packages for specific business functions and computer courseware for elementary, secondary, and college classrooms. These software materials include computer literacy, science, social science, mathematics, business, economics, accounting and engineering. Its new "basal" programs are educational pre-packs for children from kindergarten through sixth grade; their use is spreading through Canadian and Australian schoolrooms and into Third World countries. The Arabic-language publishing program has dramatically enlarged. *The Encyclopedia of Science and Technology* is on its way—electronically—to provide, via computer, current reports on single subjects.

Control Data Corporation, which may be the Goliath of the software world, stresses that "when you add applications programs to a computer system you get still more value added," and William Norris' strong advocate leadership emphasizes that CDC is in the business of knowledge services. He built the company to meet social needs, not "wants," a distinction he makes very clear; and above all it is to reform—if not save—America's school system and restore America's competitive edge in the international economy. There is no sense, he says, investing "heavily in an outmoded educational system" that makes little use of advanced technology in the teaching process.[5]

Having spent 20 years and $900 million on its PLATO computer-based education, CDC today has the first two years of the college curriculum in sciences and engineering. For the remaining college years, focus is toward math, science, and computer science. At the University of Delaware, however, a total PLATO curriculum for the four years of general studies is in place, but it is not widely available elsewhere. CDC has Fair Break job readiness programs across the country, remedial reading, math and grammar for third to eighth grade levels, secondary school courses in science, language, social studies and math. PLATO is extensive both in the number of course offerings and in the geographic regions of the world it reaches.

The content quality of CDC's higher education courses is difficult to fault: University of Illinois faculty have provided material for the great majority, some courseware in physics comes from the University of Colorado, and Southern Methodist University has developed financial management programming. Courses available go well beyond business and science to include Russian, French and other modern languages, and even New Testament Greek for Beginners, music and other humanistic studies. Computer programming instruction is offered so that teachers may create their own partial or full course software.

When testifying to Control Data's cooperative arrangements with the California State University system and more than 200 colleges and universities, Norris concedes that there may be cause for hope of their acceptance of the computer in the educational process. Recalling that "history tells us that 200 years went by after the book was introduced before it was used by teachers," he finds present utilization remarkable, although still slow.[6] Norris' ultimate goal is teaching in the broadest sense—creating knowledge, applying knowledge, and, finally, developing high quality human resource capital.

The range of implications of a learning industry with such power to assemble, store, retrieve and communicate information is manifestly profound. This is the milieu of the modern corporate classroom; it is just becoming the milieu of higher education and the adult learner equipped with the latest microcomputer technology. Industry has given us entirely new ways to handle knowledge, and the importance of college and university participation in the learning business cannot be overstressed.

New types of alignment are apparent. Members of the Apple University Consortium, using Apple computers, are required to develop software as part of the arrangement that makes the computers available for use. The plan is for students and faculty to develop curriculum and new applications for the machines. The project is proving successful; eight campuses have presented preliminary designs for a variety of new educational products. Results of the schools' research are expected early in 1985.

A most promising collaboration, "Project Athena," is underway at the Massachusetts Institute of Technology, funded jointly by $50 million in equipment and personnel from Digital Equipment Corporation and International Business Machines Corporation. MIT hopes to develop software that will transfer from one company's system to the other's and vice versa. Paul E. Gray, the university's president, states: "Athena will integrate computers into the educational environment in all fields of study throughout the university in ways which encourage new conceptual and intuitive understanding in our students."[7] Digital's equipment will be used primarily in engineering, and IBM's will go to other departments of the university. Products will be essentially educational materials to improve curricula.

IBM has arrangements also with Carnegie-Mellon and other institutions, Digital with Stevens Institute of Technology and the University of Rochester and so on. Contacts that have often been hard to establish between business and higher education—for their classrooms—are now coming about through technologies. Of course, colleges and universities are a big potential market for computer sales, and students will remember their college "machine" later when purchasing their own for home or business use. At the same time, however, the potential for faculty contribution to software instruction is great; it could be most beneficial to the quality of goods at the learning store.

The imperative is for the best teachers to create instruction of highest quality; they dare not leave the medium only to entrepreneurs and industry with skilled marketing to introduce educational courses onto the campus, schools, and homes of America and the world. That prospect offers an alarming vision of what people may be learning about history, art, social sciences, literature or any other subject.

Fortunately, some faculty are seizing the opportunity to collaborate with technical assistants or they are developing their own materials to create educational courseware. Signs are favorable. Others, however, seem loathe to accept the gauntlet, perhaps because they do not know how to do it and fear revealing their ignorance; perhaps they recall that promises for TV instruction and other hardware aids proved to be more glowing than realistic. Still others may sense the difficulties in creating a course on John Milton for the microcomputer. Some subject matter presents considerably greater challenge than quantitative or sequential learning. But, this time, the medium or technical conveyance is very different: it is interactive and flexible with a splendid memory and speed; it is affordable and convenient for assistance in yet untold ways.

Alan Kay, in a 1984 software-only issue of *Scientific American*, puts it poetically and suggests a familiar analogy:

> Computers are to computing as instruments are to music. Software is the score, whose interpretation amplifies our reach and lifts our spirits, Leonardo da Vinci called music, "the shaping of the invisible," and his phrase is even more apt as a description of software. As in the case of music, the invisibility of software is no more mysterious than where your lap goes when you stand up. The true mystery . . . is how so much can be accomplished with the simplest of materials, given the right architecture.[8]

It is possible that reluctant faculty may find computer literacy sufficiently intriguing to learn the art of writing their own scores for teaching. "As in all the arts, a romance with the material must be well under way," Kay continues. "If we value lifelong learning of arts and letters as a springboard for personal and societal growth, should any less effort be spent to make computing a part of our lives?"

Those are words of a devotee to the microcomputer, but also one who realizes the vital need for quality if the technology is to be used well for instructional benefit. Literally thousands of software products are on store shelves for sale. Organizations offer to assist us in selecting quality; critical reviews appear, boards for evaluation are available; one group associated with Consumers Union finds five out of 100 programs appraised have "quality" as judged by student appeal and varied levels of difficulty.

Some may remember the slogan, "Technology is the answer . . . but what was the question?" The educational value—the quality—is the question that will determine whether technology will be an effective tool in the learning process. While the outcome remains unknown, the process is underway and, happily, growing numbers of teachers are beginning to work with course materials. So bridges of a different sort are constructed between educators and business. Classrooms in both systems and the adult market generally may be the beneficiaries.

132

A COMPREHENSIVE VIEW

What is needed is a comprehensive analysis of the contributions and programs of the various providers—the corporate educational system, higher education, the exploding learning industry, labor and government training programs, and community resources that this report obviously could not include. Alternative systems are plentiful and delivery methods available to reach many more people. A new era has been inaugurated and calls for a review of resources with their increased possibilities.

Continuing education at any time in life has become a fact of life. Adult registration in "organized" courses suggests that some 21 million are studying part time. Most are enrolled in community colleges, four-year colleges, and universities, and their courses usually relate to job preparation: business, engineering and technology, and health sciences. The majority are already professional and technical workers, clerical, or managerial and administrative personnel. Nevertheless, many others take courses of a more general, liberal arts nature for their personal enrichment. Adults account for the greatest growth in higher education enrollment at the present time.

Corporate classrooms, as extensive and effective as they are, may offer training to some eight million adults, but that is still less than one-tenth of the total work force. All those other workers in new and old small firms need training and do not have built-in facilities or networks. Not all larger industries have strong educational programs, and the leading large firms described here are still reaching relatively small percentages of their thousands of employees. With all the contributors and alternative systems available, programs remain insufficient and unplanned in terms of total needs; they are not geared to projections for next developments and jobs in the unfolding technological age.

Who or what combination of resources will supply the adult learner and develop the abilities our nation must have not just to maintain its economic position but to dramatically improve it in the face of worldwide competition and worldwide needs? What types of training and education are essential both for individual Americans and for the nation's imper-

133

atives? Which of our resources are most suitable to assist and should be rallied to help in providing the necessary programs? To restore America's leadership position solidly from its educational and training base requires the broadest assessment of the problem areas that undermine productivity and drain the human energy resources of the nation.

Training and retraining workers is a major challenge with complicated dimensions. Older industries' decline and automation and robotics entering factory floors have taken a human toll of over eight million. For many able and willing workers, the revolution in manufacturing processes creates a yawning chasm. For others—disadvantaged or illiterate—who never made it to the factory floor, the chasm is endless. Well-conceived and implemented training programs could release an energy potential and raise productivity levels to the benefit of our society—and offset welfare costs.

Technological advancement and change have characterized the workplace since the late eighteenth century when Eli Whitney's cotton gin and Wilkinson's machine to make machines appeared. Since then the harnessing of electricity and utilization of the internal combustion engine early in this century, and now the computer with its innovations have all brought fundamental changes in the tools and other materials used to perform work.

The misfit between workers' capabilities and the technological skills required to do the work has been deplored since mass production and centralized factories signaled the first salvos of the Industrial Revolution 200 years ago. Through three "work" revolutions within two centuries, since the early days of the great Lowell textile mills, companies have largely provided their own education for adjustment and have urged vocational training and support services from other educational sources. Often, on-the-job training was adequate with or without additional organized instruction; today worker dislocation is more complicated.

Although the old cyclical trend of technological advancement and educational retooling continues, this time around demands are accelerating. The last 30 years have brought increased speed of change and greater differentiation in skills and abilities needed for knowledge-intensive job applications. It has been pointed out repeatedly that there is a dangerous

134

and widening gulf between the very smart and the not-so-smart employee. The blue collar worker's job is at stake. Never before have new jobs and retraining been so immediately crucial. Product, production method, and "career" obsolescence are rapid and may be repeated several times within an individual's work life.

When a corporation's philosophy embraces lifetime employment for workers and advocates promotion from within, job retraining and adjustment become a corporate responsibility. Companies like IBM and Hewlett-Packard are so committed and have their own extensive training programs. But these are giant multinationals at the forefront in a growing and expanding industry. Other companies, even those so situated, are less far-sighted and do not protect their workers, often to the company's detriment in the long run. They are the ones who cut-and-run on quick glances at the bottom line. For whatever reason, persons are displaced and potential productivity for society is being lost.

Earlier economic revolutions found answers in stimulating the new industries that brought new jobs and types of employment. Big changes create additional fields; they don't just eliminate jobs. This process is underway again but the questions remain: Will such natural processes provide enough jobs, and of what kinds? The new worlds of "service" and "information" companies have been emerging for some time and have now absorbed nearly 80 percent of the work force. High tech, to an often overlooked extent, has permeated the conventional smokestack industries. And it has already invaded older established communications, offices, entertainment, and health care fields—in each case beginning new processes and products that have brought their own demands along with them.

Some predictions for greatest employment target sales jobs for an increase of almost 19 percent, or more than one million, by 1990 according to the Bureau of Labor Statistics. And there will also be many walk-in health care centers, for example, where the main service will be provided by technicians and their computer-assisted diagnostic equipment. Although real job growth will not be computer or electronic industries themselves, fresh openings will come in businesses using the technologies. Programmers are needed in the cable industry, for example. New small

135

companies will grow and "cottage" industries taking full advantage of modems for computer telecommunications are springing up.

Regardless of the jobs born of the computer and its accessories, this third revolution is not synchronized with the begetting of sufficient new jobs naturally because of its "knowledge-intensive" nature. A new and different type of retraining is called for—more specific, informed and sophisticated. It is learning of a higher order for understanding conceptual bases essential to the operational control and utilization of information systems. Educational demands of such magnitude require human flexibility and trainability and, as with other complex problems, solutions rest on perceptive, thoughtful policies implemented on a comprehensive basis for practical results.

Corporate classrooms could contribute the most to comprehensive retraining programs under present circumstances: their methods and style are particularly appropriate and their knowledge of the skills needed for work in spin-off fields most pertinent. But the burden can not, and should not, be placed solely on industry's doorstep. Such default by policy-makers and educators would not be for the good of the country or its economic health. If the corporate model—with technical advice and expertise—were replicated and transferred to other sectors, the pattern could be appropriate and effective. Electronic educational delivery systems can reach any location; many segments of the learning industry already have instructive materials for individual study and could produce additional job training programs. Vendors transport seminar instruction, complete with a teacher and supportive materials, to wherever needed.

Community colleges are already playing an important and helpful part. Labor unions' educational programs are also involved. Government agencies' training programs from federal to local levels could be extended and coordinated along with other community resources. Four-year colleges and universities could contribute course work for some types of employment, and faculty could create software and videocassettes to teach "personally" beyond their locale.

The recent U.S. Job Training Partnership Act that went into effect in 1983 is inadequate, and funded with barely half the monies that went into the old Comprehensive Education and Training Act. Further, the new

136

program designates two-thirds of funding for vocational and on-the-job training for poor youths. That leaves $215 million for retraining some eight million workers who have lost their jobs because of recession or automation. Disadvantaged youth and displaced workers need training assistance, but funds allotted are not sufficient for both, and especially for the latter who were household providers.

One admirable element in the inadequate attempt is the involvement of business and corporate leaders in determining the kinds of training needed for persons on the state or local level. The danger is that training programs will be so directed to immediate employment and specific tasks that workers may bounce from job to job and intermittent training programs for the rest of their lives. If relatively well-trained people will change jobs maybe five times in a work life, then consider the effects of fast-fix training for the disadvantaged and currently displaced.

What is needed is vision or, at the very least, some long-range training programs that don't just "pay off" tomorrow, but benefit real education for America's future. If older industries are criticized for short-sightedly taking profits instead of reinvesting for capital improvements and long-range development, are we doing any better in investment policies in the major resource for the knowledge-intensive world: namely, its human resources for production and its research capacity for new applications and future markets?

Broad scale programs are needed for our country's future, and education—both in corporate classrooms and schoolrooms—is inevitably a large part of any such attempt. Strategic development for the long term is essential. Leadership and sustained effort to support and finance basic programs are too often missing. The Heritage Foundation's *Blueprint for Jobs and Industrial Growth* asks competitive markets to solve problems: competition between public and private schools through voucher systems or tax credits or competition between teachers by pay scales "that reflect supply and demand" in subjects according to market conditions. Business is encouraged to work with schools, but no comprehensive programs are suggested.

In search of a better approach to economic development in the nation, the Business-Higher Education Forum in 1983 submitted proposals to the

President. A Commission on Industrial Competitiveness was named, including three corporate leaders along with representatives from labor organizations and academic institutions. The commission prepared recommendations on human resources, capital resources, research, development and manufacturing, and international trade. Connections to academic education dealt primarily with vocational-technical schools, and business and engineering in traditional higher education. But the commission's authorization expired at the end of 1984, having had little more than a year in which to probe complicated issues and consider masses of information.

Global Stakes' authors argue cogently for a Presidential Commission on Technology and Productivity. They call for a new High Technology Morrill Act to do for the United States today what the original nineteenth century Morrill Act did to assist agricultural and industrial progress. At that time the government took its first big step into subsidizing the education that became the basis for an informed citizenry and workers that were able to introduce and cope with the next industrial revolution.

Today, such bold action is needed once again, the authors argue, as a collaborative effort involving universities, industry, and research to lead this country in economic development. The proposed High-Tech Morrill Act addresses four national economic policy needs: sustained financial support to the American system of education, lifelong learning, high school incentives, and a global view of technology.

Their proposal, of course, stresses science and technology, and especially engineering. They ask for federal leadership and national policy, and they call for a strong educational system. The future of this country is inextricably tied to the future of high technology and to the quality of our education.

Their High-Tech Morrill Act achieved recognition to the point of combination in a triple bill for aid to engineering and science with math development at the lower levels of schools; the bill remains in oblivion with a $500 million request for the total job. That is a parody of the original, far-sighted Morrill Act, but as the authors patiently suggest, it took a decade to get the original land grant legislation. One wonders today

138

if our country can wait a decade for a new national commitment to education.

The time has come to take the larger view on a sustained basis. We do not suggest another presidential commission with short life and limited impact, nor do we propose legislative initiative with token funds to improve temporarily the patient's symptoms. Rather, what is needed is an ongoing concern with a broader mandate. It is more than just our competitive position; it is the health of our nation at stake.

Could we not consider a *Strategic Council for Educational Development* that would help guide improvement and national policies for the next decade? Without such continuing leadership no one scheme will suffice. Too many tactical proposals and short-range programs are being offered. The debate must move forward, and society must make the long-range capital investment in human resources and their development for the future of individuals and the national economy. Very often when education programs have been started or promoted in our country there has been an economic purpose—the progress of America seen by Horace Mann and Horace Greeley or the legislators who passed the Morrill Act.

Once again we need vision and leadership to project programs for emerging needs. The new vision is one of continuing education for national renewal and the pursuit of well-being for all citizens in a period of dramatic technological change. The council would consider national needs for the foreseeable future and propose a variety of means and alternative ways to meet them. Basic to its deliberations is the improvement of education given by all sectors and the coordination of programs among them to increase the effectiveness of total opportunities.

The Strategic Council would have a three-fold purpose:

> *To assess the nation's emerging educational needs.* The focus will be on training needs: retraining displaced workers, training the disadvantaged and illiterate, upgrading scientific and technological training coordinated with high tech projections and natural resource development. Educational needs must be evaluated in the context of lifelong learning with training required at periodic intervals as well as increased opportunities for an aging population.

139

To identify and review our educational resources. The focus will be on the different education sectors and how they relate to one another. The roles of schools and colleges and adult education will be evaluated along with corporate education. Training programs of labor, government agencies and the military also are vital to the review. Finally, educational opportunities must be assessed with the new technologies and delivery systems in mind and with the instructional materials coming from the learning industry.

To recommend policies and programs. Drawing on our extensive educational resources, proposals will suggest how programs can be designed to meet more effectively the crucial needs of our society in a new era. The goal here is not to establish a national manpower policy, which has never been effective in the United States; rather, the challenge is to give guidance to the public and private sectors, to suggest strategies for federal and state action, and to identify ways in which colleges and the corporate sector can cooperatively serve the lifelong education of adults. Council reports may be viewed as forecasts that bring intelligence to bear on complex problems and counsel adjustments and new programs and policies as required.

We recognize, of course, the risks involved in comprehensive planning. And we know that past experiments have usually had only marginal success. Still the effort must be made to benefit from past errors and do it better this time.

Urging the restoration of America's leadership and competitive position in the world economy sounds hollow if our educational resources are ignored as the underpinning for development and if our training needs go unmet. The nation is weakened by every person unable to contribute to its productivity and enrichment in every sense.

The challenge is to create a pool of well-skilled and educated citizens from which society's requirements—including the economic—can be met for the future. Concerted action is called for from industry, labor, schools and universities, and the federal government. Such planning and projections cannot come effectively from separate states; their role comes in implementing and adjusting the programs within a great nation. No mat-

140

ter how appealing the new federalism may be, it abdicates leadership for America as a whole.

Our country has the pattern of strategic planning bodies for the most crucial and complicated problems of national defense and security. Is it not possible to have the most basic operation of all—a Strategic Council for Educational Development in the United States? The elements are in place and all would welcome the guidance and endorse the support of national policies and leadership. Americans have a generic belief in education, as they should, in terms of the record.

NOTES

CHAPTER I.

1. Botkin, James, Dan Dimancescu, and Ray Stata, with John McClellan. *Global Stakes: The Future of High Technology in America* (Cambridge, Mass.: Ballinger, 1982), p. 183.
2. *Ibid.*, pp. 7-8.
3. McKenzie, Richard B., ed. *A Blueprint for Jobs and Industrial Growth* (Washington, D.C.: Heritage Foundation, 1984), pp. 44-48.
4. Freeman, Roger A. "Pursuit of Excellence? The Income and Outcome of Education" in Moore (ed.), *To Promote Prosperity*, pp. 319-341.
5. Peters, Thomas J., and Robert H. Waterman, Jr. *In Search of Excellence: Lessons from America's Best Run Companies* (New York: Harper & Row, 1982), and Levering, Robert, Milton Moskowitz, and Michael Katz. *The 100 Best Companies to Work for in America* (Reading, Mass.: Addison-Wesley, 1984).
6. Quoted by Martin E. Smith, "Training Costs Accounting at New England Telephone" in *The Nature and Extent of Employee Training and Development: A State of the Art Forum on Data Gathering*, p. 134.
7. Gilbert, Thomas F. "Training: The $100 Billion Opportunity" *Training and Development Journal*, November 1976, pp. 3-8.
8. Hodgkinson, Harold, in Gerald G. Gold (ed.), *Business and Higher Education: Toward New Alliances* (San Francisco: Jossey-Bass, 1981), p. 1.
9. Henry, James F. "Report of the First Steering Committee Meeting, Human Resources Executive Program" issued by the Center for Public Resources (New York City, 1981), p. 2.
10. Goldstein, Harold. "Using Data on Employee Training from the Survey of Participation in Adult Education (Current Population Survey)" in *The Nature and Extent of Employee Training and Development*, pp. 167-176.
11. *Ibid.*, p. 171. The reference is to a study being conducted by the Doctoral Program on Public Policy at George Washington University.
12. *Ibid.*, pp. 171-172.
13. *Ibid.*, p. 173.
14. Smith, "Training Costs Accounting" p. 134.
15. Luxenberg, Stan. "Education at AT&T" *Change*, December-January, 1978-79, pp. 27-35.
16. Greenwald, John. "The Colossus That Works," *Time*, July 11, 1983, p. 47.
17. Psychological Associates, Inc. "Executive Survey: Impact of Economy on Training

Budgets, 1982" and "Executive Survey: 1983 T&D Plans and Budgets Finalized." The survey went to 90 major U.S. companies of the following types: 50 percent manufacturing, 20 percent finance and insurance, 20 percent wholesale, retail and service, and 10 percent transportation, communications, utilities (Standard Industrial Code classification).

18. "U.S. Training Census and Trends Report, 1982." *Training, HRD*, October 1982, pp. 16-90.

19. DeCarlo, Charles R., and Ormsbee W. Robinson. *Education in Business and Industry* (New York: Center for Applied Research in Education, 1966) pp. 10, 11.

20. Taubman, Philip. "Telephone Unions Back Bell Offer; Strike's End Seen" *The New York Times*, August 22, 1983, p. A19.

21. Cross, K. Patricia. "New Frontiers for Higher Education: Business and the Professions" *Current Issues in Higher Education*, No. 3, Washington, D.C., 1981, pp. 1-7.

22. Lynton, Ernest A. *The Missing Connection Between Business and Education* (New York: Macmillan, 1984), Ch. 4.

23. Eliason, Carol. "Small Business, Big Opportunities" *Community and Junior College Journal*, December/January, 1982-83, pp. 32-34.

24. Bruce, James D., William Siebert, Louis Smullin, and Robert Fano. *Lifelong Cooperative Education. Report of the Centennial Study Committee, Massachusetts Institute of Technology, Department of Electrical Engineering and Computer Science* (Cambridge, Mass.: M.I.T., October 2, 1982) pp. 6-11.

25. *The Washington Post*, November 20, 1984, p. D2. The report is from The Council for Financial Aid to Education.

26. "Participation in Adult Education, May, 1981," issued by NCES, June 1982.

27. *Future Directions for a Learning Society: Annotated Bibliography of Publications and Background Papers 1977-1980* (New York: The College Entrance Examination Board, 1980). Figures are based on 1978 reports.

CHAPTER II.

1. Boorstin, Daniel J. *The Americans: The National Experience* (New York: Random House, 1965) p. 30.

2. Hall, Richard H. *Occupations and the Social Structure* (Englewood Cliffs, N.J.: Prentice-Hall, 1969) Ch. 2.

3. Robinson, Donald R. *Spotlight on a Union: The Story of the United Hatters, Cap and Millinery Workers International Union* (New York: Dial, 1948) p. 38.

4. Purcell, Richard J. *Connecticut in Transition: 1775-1818* (Middletown, Ct.: Wesleyan University Press, 1963) p. 82; and Roth, Matthew, and others. *Connecticut: An Inventory of Historic Engineering and Industrial Sites* (Washington, D.C.: Society for Industrial Archaeology, 1981) p. 240.

5. Dulles, Foster Rhea. *Labor in America* (New York: Crowell, 1955) p. 74.

6. *Ibid.*, p. 73.

7. Cable, Mary. *American Manners and Morals* (New York: American Heritage, 1969) p. 94.

8. Dulles, *Labor in America*, p. 74.
9. Darby, William, and Theodore Dwight, Jr. *A New Gazetteer of the United States of America* (Hartford, Ct.: Edward Hopkins, 1833) p. 268.
10. Quoted in Holbrook, Stewart H. *The Yankee Exodus: An Account of Migration from New England* (Seattle: University of Washington Press, 1950) p. 6.
11. Dulles, *Labor in America*, pp. 74, 75.
12. Fisher, Bernice M. *Industrial Education: American Ideals and Institutions* (Madison, Wisc.: University of Wisconsin Press, 1967) p. 10.
13. *Ibid.*, p. 22.
14. Quoted by Beard, Charles A., and Mary R. *A Basic History of the United States* (New York: New Home Library, 1944) p. 237.
15. Platt, Nathaniel, and Muriel Jean Drummond. *Our Nation from its Creation: A Great Experiment* (Englewood Cliffs, N.J.: Prenctice-Hall, 1965) pp. 431, 432.
16. Cremin, Lawrence A. *The Transformation of the School* (New York: Vintage, 1964) pp. 24-26.
17. *Ibid.*, pp. 26-28.
18. McCauley, Elfrieda B. "The New England Mill Girls: Feminine Influence in the Development of Public Libraries in New England, 1820-1860" (unpublished DLS thesis, Columbia University, 1971) p. 259.
19. Roth, Matthew, and others. *Connecticut: An Inventory of Historic Engineering and Industrial Sites*, pp. 42-43.
20. Beard, Charles A. and Mary R. *A Basic History of the United States*, pp. 749-750.
21. Cremin, *Transformation of the School*, pp. 50-51.
22. "Business," in Beard, Charles A. (ed.) *Whither Mankind: A Panorama of Modern Civilization* (New York: Longmans, 1928) p. 103.
23. Clark, Harold F., and Harold S. Sloan. *Classrooms in the Factories* (New York: Fairleigh Dickinson University Press, 1958) pp. 6, 7.
24. Wilhelm, Donald "The 'Big Business' Man as a Social Worker" in *The Outlook*, 108, October 28, 1914, pp. 496-500. The quotation is in Jeanette S. Baker, "An Analysis of Degree Programs Offered by Selected Industrial Corporations" (unpublished dissertation, University of Arizona, 1983).
25. "History of American Management Association" (unpublished manuscript, New York: Archives of AMA). This is a primary source of facts concerning the National Association of Corporation Schools.
26. Clark and Sloan, *Classrooms in the Factories*, p. 6.
27. "History of American Management Association," n.p.
28. DeCarlo, Charles R., and Ormsbee W. Robinson. *Education in Business and Industry* (New York: Center for Applied Research in Education, 1966) pp. 6, 7.
29. *Ibid.*, p. 8.
30. Clark and Sloan, *Classrooms in the Factories*, p. 3; Serbein, Oscar N., *Educational Activities of Business* (Washington, D.C.: American Council on Education, 1961).
31. Clark and Sloan, *Classrooms in the Factories*, p. 3. In 1956 average institutional cost per student for a four-year course in American colleges and universities was about $4,000 (U.S. Bureau of the Census, *Statistical Abstract of the United States: 1981* 102d edition—Washington, D.C., 1981).

32. *Ibid.*, pp. 15-16.
33. Galbraith, John Kenneth. *The New Industrial State* (Boston: Houghton Mifflin, 1967) p. 243.
34. Bowden, G. T. and R. K. Greenleaf. *The Study of the Humanities as an Approach to Executive Development* (privately printed, Bell System, circa early 1970s), p. 7.
35. *Ibid.*, p. 10.
36. Beard, ed. *Whither Mankind*, p. 370.

CHAPTER III.

1. Forrester, Jay W. "A New Corporate Design" *Industrial Management Review*, Fall 1965, pp. 5-17.
2. Watkins, Beverly T. "Higher Education Now Big Business for Big Business" *The Chronicle of Higher Education*, April 13, 1983, pp. 1, 6.
3. "Dana University—Offering Unique Industrial Training at Dana Corporation" *Training and Development Journal*, March 1977, pp. 46-48.
4. Whitlock, Suzanne. *Education Programs in Industry: Case Studies—IBM Entry Level Marketing Training and Rust International, Inc.* (unpublished Ph.D. dissertation, The University of Alabama, 1982). This is an interesting history of IBM's entry-level marketing training based on several IBM publications and interviews with staff and officers in the division.
5. Reif, F. "Educational Challenges for the University" *Science*, May 3, 1974, pp. 537-542.
6. Eddy, Bob, and John Kellow. "What We've Learned About Learning—A Corporate 'University' at Leeds & Northrup Co." *Training and Development Journal*, May 1977, pp. 32-38.

CHAPTER IV.

1. Henry, James F. and Susan Raymond, "Basic Skills in the U.S. Work Force: The Contrasting Perceptions of Business, Labor, and Public Education" (New York: The Center for Public Resources, 1983).
2. *Ibid.*, p. 24.
3. Rhodes, Lucien. "The Passion of Robert Swiggett," *INC.* April, 1984, p. 139.
4. Lusterman, Seymour. *Managerial Competence: The Public Affairs Aspects* (New York: The Conference Board, 1981) Report no. 805, pp. iv-v.
5. Remarks reported in Business-Higher Education Forum, "Highlights of the Winter (Washington, D.C.: American Council on Education). 1984 Meeting."
6. Tsurumi, Yoshi. "Too Many U.S. Managers are Technologically Illiterate" *High Technology*, April 1984, pp. 14, 16.
7. *The New York Times*, March 4, 1984, pp. D1, 11.
8. Pitre, Lee Frances. *Credit and Non-Credit Education Opportunities Offered by Large Industrial Corporations* (unpublished Ph.D. dissertation, The University of Texas, 1980) p. 81.

146

9. *Ibid.*, p. 73.

10. Whitlock, Suzanne. *Education Programs in Industry: Case Studies—IBM Entry Level Marketing Training and Rust International Inc.* (unpublished Ph.D. dissertation, The University of Alabama, 1982) p. 93.

11. Quoted in Botkin, James, Dan Dimancescu, and Ray Stata, with John McClellan. *Global Stakes: The Future of High Technology in America* (Cambridge, Mass.: Ballinger, 1982) p. 19.

12. Botkin, and others, *Global Stakes*, pp. 20-21.

13. Pitre, *Credit and Non-Credit Education*, p. 82.

14. Baker, Jeanette Sledge. "An Analysis of Degree Programs Offered by Selected Industrial Corporations" (unpublished Ph.D. dissertation, University of Arizona, 1983).

CHAPTER V.

1. *The New York Times*, May 9, 1983, p. A5.

2. Baker, Jeanette Sledge. "An Analysis of Degree Programs Offered by Selected Industrial Corporations" (unpublished Ph.D. dissertation, University of Arizona, 1983).

3. Hawthorne, Elizabeth M., Patricia A. Libby, and Nancy S. Nash. "The Emergence of Corporate Colleges." *The Journal of Continuing Higher Education*, Fall 1983, pp. 2-9. The authors identified fourteen such "corporate colleges." Five are added here to update and facts are corrected.

4. Betters-Reed, Bonita Lynn. "A History and Analysis of Three Innovative Graduate Institutions: The Arthur D. Little Management Education Institute, The Massachusetts General Hospital Institute of Health Professions, and The Wang Institute of Graduate Studies" (unpublished Ph.D. dissertation, Boston College, 1982).

5. *The New York Times*, July 26, 1984, pp. D1, 5.

6. *Mass High Tech* (Newspaper), February 20-March 4, 1984, p. 17.

7. *The New York Times*, April 17, 1984, p. C7.

8. Betters-Reed, "A History and Analysis of Three Innovative Graduate Institutions," pp. 96-109.

9. *Ibid.*, p. 72ff.

CHAPTER VI.

1. Branscomb, Lewis M., and Paul C. Gilmore. "Education in Private Industry" *Daedalus: American Higher Education: Toward an Uncertain Future* (Cambridge, Mass.: American Academy of Arts and Sciences, Winter, 1975) pp. 231-232.

2. "Independent Labs Scramble to Catch Up with the New Technologies" *Business Week*, September 10, 1984, pp. 66-75.

3. *The New York Times*, December 3, 1984, pp. A1, B6.

4. *The New York Times*, September 1, 1984, p. 33.

5. Norris, William C. *Human Capital: The Profitable Investment* Series no. 19. (St.

Paul, Minn.: Control Data Corporation, October 1982) p. 2. This address was given to the annual meeting of the American Association of State Colleges and Universities.

6. *Ibid.*, p. 7.
7. *The New York Times*, June 1, 1983, p. D20.
8. Kay, Alan. "Computer Software" *Scientific American*, September 1984, pp. 53-59.

SELECTED BIBLIOGRAPHY

Anderson, Richard E. and Elizabeth Swain Kasl. *The Costs and Financing of Adult Education and Training* (Lexington, Mass.: Lexington Books, 1982).

Aslanian, Carol B. and Henry M. Brickell. *Americans in Transition: Life Changes as Reasons for Adult Learning* (New York: College Entrance Examination Board, 1980).

Baker, H. Kent. "Education and Training Programs of Financial Trade Associations" *Phi Delta Kappan*, January 1980, 319-321.

Baker, Jeanette Sledge. "An Analysis of Degree Programs Offered by Selected Industrial Corporations" (unpub. diss., University of Arizona, 1983).

Beard, Charles A. *American Government and Politics.* Rev. ed. (New York: Macmillan, 1915).

Beard, Charles A., ed. *Whither Mankind: A Panorama of Modern Civilization* (New York: Longmans, 1928).

Beard, Charles A. and Mary R. *A Basic History of the United States* (New York: New Home Library, 1944).

Beck, Robert E. "The Liberal Arts Major in Bell System Management" (paper presented to the Association of American Colleges, March 4, 1981).

Berg, Ivar, ed. *Human Resources and Economic Welfare* (New York: Columbia, 1972).

Betters-Reed, Bonita Lynn. "A History and Analysis of Three Innovative Graduate Institutions: The Arthur D. Little Management Education Institute, The Massachusetts General Hospital Institute of Health Professions, and The Wang Institute of Graduate Studies" (unpub. diss., Boston College, 1982).

Boorstin, Daniel J. *The Americans: The National Experience* (New York: Random House, 1965).

Botkin, James, Dan Dimancescu, and Ray Stata, with John McClellan. *Global Stakes: The Future of High Technology in America* (Cambridge, Mass.: Ballinger, 1982).

Bowden, G. T. and R. K. Greenleaf. *The Study of the Humanities as an Approach to Executive Development* (privately printed, Bell System, circa early 1970s).

Branscomb, Lewis M. and Paul C. Gilmore. "Education in Private Industry" *Daedalus: American Higher Education: Toward an Uncertain Future* (Cambridge, Mass.: American Academy of Arts and Sciences, Winter 1975), 222-233.

Bruce, James D., William Siebert, Louis Smullin, and Robert Fano. *Lifelong Cooperative Education. Report of the Centennial Study Committee, Massachusetts Institute of Technology, Department of Electrical Engineering and Computer Science* (Cambridge, Mass.: M.I.T., October 2, 1982).

"Business and Universities: A New Partnership" *Business Week*, Dec. 20, 1982, 58-61.

Business-Higher Education Forum. *America's Competitive Challenge: The Need for a National Response* A report to the President of the United States (Washington, D.C.: American Council on Education, 1983).

Business-Higher Education Forum. *Highlights of the Winter 1984 Meeting* (Washington, D.C.: American Council on Education).

Cable, Mary. *American Manners and Morals* (New York: American Heritage, 1969).

Carnevale, Anthony P. *Human Capital: A High Yield Corporate Investment: Executive Summary* (Washington, D.C.: American Society for Training and Development, 1982).

Carnevale, Anthony P., and Harold Goldstein. *Employee Training: Its Changing Role and an Analysis of New Data* (Washington, D.C.: ASTD Press, 1983).

Chamberlin, Neil W. "The Corporation as a College" *Atlantic Monthly*, June 1965, 102-104.

Chapin, William C. *Statement of the Pacific Mills, Presented to the Special Jury of the Paris Exposition of 1867* (Lawrence, Mass.: Geo. S. Merrill, 1868).

Clark, Harold F. and Harold S. Sloan. *Classrooms in the Factories* (New York: Fairleigh Dickinson University Press, 1958).

Coles, James S. *Technological Innovation in the '80s* (Englewood Cliffs, N.J.: Prentice-Hall, 1984).

"Company Courses Go Collegiate." *Business Week*, February 26, 1979, 90, 92.

"Corporations Bet on Campus R&D." *Business Week*, Dec. 20, 1982, 61-62.

Corrigan, Gary. "Corporate Training: A Career for Teachers?" *Phi Delta Kappan*, January 1980, 328-331.

Craig, Robert L. and Christine J. Evers. "Employers as Educators: The 'Shadow Education System' " *Business and Higher Education: Toward New Alliances* (San Francisco: Jossey-Bass, 1981) 29-46.

Cremin, Lawrence A. *The Transformation of the School* (New York: Vintage, 1964).

Cross, K. Patricia. "New Frontiers for Higher Education: Business and the Professions" *Current Issues in Higher Education*, no. 3, Washington, D.C., 1981, 1-7.

"Dana University—Offering Unique Industrial Training at Dana Corporation" *Training and Development Journal*, March 1977, 46-48.

150

Darby, William, and Theodore Dwight, Jr. *A New Gazetteer of the United States of America* (Hartford, Ct.: Edward Hopkins, 1833).

Dean, Peter. "Education and Training at IBM" *Phi Delta Kappan*, January 1980, 317-318.

DeCarlo, Charles R., and Ormsbee W. Robinson. *Education in Business and Industry* (New York: Center for Applied Research in Education, 1966).

Doll, Russell. "Speculations on the Meaning of the Trend Toward Corporate Education" *Phi Delta Kappan*, January 1980, 333-337.

Dulles, Foster Rhea. *Labor in America* (New York: Crowell, 1955).

Eddy, Bob and John Kellow. "What We've Learned About Learning—A Corporate 'University' At Leeds & Northrup Co." *Training and Development Journal*, May 1977, 32-38.

Eliason, Carol. "Small Business, Big Opportunities" *Community and Junior College Journal*, December/January 1982-83, 32-34.

"Executive Survey: Impact of Economy on Training Budgets, 1982" and "Executive Survey: 1983 T&D Plans and Budgets Finalized." (St. Louis, Mo.: Psychological Associates, Inc., 8201 Maryland Avenue, 63105).

Fenwick, Dorothy C., ed. *Directory of Campus-Business Linkages: Education and Business Prospering Together* (New York: Macmillan, 1983).

Fisher, Bernice M. *Industrial Education: American Ideals and Institutions* (Madison, Wisc.: University of Wisconsin Press, 1967).

Forrester, J. W. "A New Corporate Design" *Industrial Management Review*, Fall 1965, 5-17.

The Fourth Revolution: Instructional Technology in Higher Education. A Report by The Carnegie Commission on Higher Education (New York: McGraw-Hill, 1972).

Future Directions For A Learning Society: Annotated Bibliography of Publications and Background Papers 1977-1980 (New York: The College Entrance Examination Board, 1980).

Galbraith, John Kenneth. *The New Industrial State* (Boston: Houghton Mifflin, 1967).

Gilbert, Thomas F. "The High Cost of Knowledge" *Personnel*, March-April 1976, 11-23.

Gilbert, Thomas F. "Training: The $100 Billion Opportunity" *Training and Development Journal*, November 1976, 3-8.

Gold, Gerard G., ed. *Business and Higher Education: Toward New Alliances* (San Francisco: Jossey-Bass, 1981).

Greenwald, John. "The Colossus That Works" *Time*, July 11, 1983, 44-54.

A Guide to Educational Programs in Noncollegiate Organizations (Albany, N.Y.: The University of the State of New York, 1980, 1982).

Hall, Richard H. *Occupations and the Social Structure* (Englewood cliffs, N.J.: Prentice-Hall, 1969).

Harbison, Frederick H. "Human Resources as the Wealth of Nations" in Berg, Ivar (ed.) *Human Resources and Economic Welfare* (New York: Columbia University Press, 1972).

Hawthorne, Elizabeth M., Patricia A. Libby, and Nancy S. Nash. "The Emergence of Corporate Colleges" *The Journal of Continuing Higher Education*, Fall 1983, 2-9. The article was developed from a dissertation abstract, University of Michigan, 1982.

Henry, James F. "Report of the First Steering Committee Meeting, Human Resources Executive Program" (New York: The Center for Public Resources, 1981).

Henry, James F., and Susan Raymond. "Basic Skills in the U.S. Work Force: The Contrasting Perceptions of Business, Labor, and Public Education" (New York: The Center for Public Resources, 1983).

"History of American Management Associations" (MS [circa 1925]). Archives of the American Management Associations, New York. A partial restatement by W. H. Lange is "The American Management Association and Its Predecessors." Special Paper: No. 17. (Archives of The American Management Associations, New York, 1928).

Hodgkinson, Harold, in Gold, Gerald G. (ed.) *Business and Higher Education: Toward New Alliances* (San Francisco: Jossey-Bass, 1981).

Holbrook, Stewart H. *The Yankee Exodus: An Account of Migration from New England* (Seattle: University of Washington Press, 1950).

Kay, Alan. "Computer Software." *Scientific American*, September 1984, 53-59.

Levenson, Anne M. *Factors Related to Establishment by Business Organizations of Courses Apparently Equivalent to Those Offered by Geographically Accessible Higher Education Institutions* (unpub. diss., University of Pittsburgh, 1983).

Levering, Robert, Milton Moskowitz, and Michael Katz. *The 100 Best Companies to Work for in America* (Reading, Mass.: Addison-Wesley, 1984).

Levien, Roger E. *The Emerging Technology: Instructional Use of the Computer in Higher Technology* (New York: McGraw-Hill, 1972).

Lusterman, Seymour. *Education in Industry*. (New York: The Conference Board, 1977). Research Report no. 719.

Lusterman, Seymour. *Managerial Competence: The Public Affairs Aspects* (New York: The Conference Board, 1981). Report no. 805.

Luxenberg, Stan. "AT&T and Citicorp: Prototypes in Job Training among Large Corporations" *Phi Delta Kappan*, January 1980, 314-316.

Luxenberg, Stan. "Education at AT&T." *Change*, December-January 1978/79, 27-35.

152

Lynton, Ernest A. "A Crisis of Purpose: Reexamining the Role of the University" *Change*, October 1983.

Lynton, Ernest A. *The Missing Connection Between Business and Education* (New York: Macmillan, 1984).

Lynton, Ernest A. "The Role of Colleges and Universities in Corporate Education and Training" (Discussion paper prepared for the Ford Foundation).

Lynton, Ernest A. "The Role of Higher Education in Human Capital Formation and Maintenance" (paper prepared for the Alden Seminar on Higher Education, Boston, 1983).

McCauley, Elfrieda B. "The New England Mill Girls: Feminine Influence in the Development of Public Libraries in New England, 1820-1860" (unpub. DLS thesis, Columbia University, 1971).

McKenzie, Richard B., ed. *A Blueprint for Jobs and Industrial Growth* (Washington, D.C.: Heritage Foundation, 1984).

McQuigg, Beverly. "The Role of Education in Industry" *Phi Delta Kappan*, January 1980, 324-325.

Maeroff, Gene I. "Business is Cutting into the Market" *The New York Times*, August 30, 1981, Survey of Continuing Education, Section 12, 1, 19.

Management Training and Development Programs. Personnel Policies Forum Survey no. 116 (Washington D.C.: Bureau of National Affairs, 1977).

Massachusetts Higher Education in the Eighties: Manpower and the Economy (The Alden Seminars, a white paper, June 1982).

Maxwell, J.F. "Who Will Provide Continuing Education for Professionals?" *AAHE Bulletin*, December 1980.

Moore, John H., ed. *To Promote Prosperity: U.S. Domestic Policy in the Mid-1980s* (Stanford: Hoover Institution Press, 1984).

The National Guide to Educational Credit for Training Programs 1980 and 1982-83 eds. (Washington, D.C.: Program on Noncollegiate Sponsored Instruction of the American Council on Education).

The Nature and Extent of Employee Training and Development: A State of the Art Forum on Data Gathering (Washington, D.C.: American Society for Training and Development, 1982).

Noble, Kenneth B. "The Corporate Halls of Ivy Grow" *The New York Times*, August 30, 1981, Survey of Continuing Education, Section 12, 21.

Norris, William C. *Human Capital: The Profitable Investment* Series no. 19 (St. Paul, Minn.: Control Data Corporation, October 1982). This address was given to the annual meeting of the American Association of State Colleges and Universities.

Peterfreund, Stanley. "Education in Industry—Today and in the Future" *Training and Development Journal*, May 1976, 30-40.

Peters, Thomas J., and Robert H. Waterman, Jr. *In Search of Excellence: Lessons from America's Best Run Companies* (New York: Harper & Row, 1982).

Pitre, Lee Frances. *Credit and Non-Credit Education Opportunities Offered by Large Industrial Corporations* (unpub. diss., The University of Texas, 1980.

Platt, Nathaniel, and Muriel Jean Drummond. *Our Nation from its Creation: A Great Experiment* (Englewood Cliffs, N.J.: Prentice-Hall, 1965).

Porter, Jack. "Corporations that Grant Degrees" *Business and Society Review*, Spring 1982, 41-46.

Purcell, Richard J. *Connecticut in Transition: 1775-1818* (Middletown, Ct.: Wesleyan University Press, 1963).

Reif, F. "Educational Challenges for the University" *Science*, May 3, 1974, 537-542.

Robinson, Donald R. *Spotlight on a Union: The Story of the United Hatters, Cap and Millinery Workers International Union* (New York: Dial, 1948).

Rockart, John Fralick, and Michael S. Scott Morton. *Computers and the Learning Process in Higher Education* (New York: McGraw-Hill, 1975).

Roth, Matthew, and others. *Connecticut: An Inventory of Historic Engineering and Industrial Sites* (Washington, D.C.: Society for Industrial Archaeology, 1981).

Schmidt, Warren and Barry Posner. *Managerial Values in Perspective* (New York: American Management Associations, 1983).

Schwaller, Anthony. "The Need for Education/Training Programs in Industry" *Phi Delta Kappan*, January 1980, 322-323.

Serbein, Oscar N. *Educational Activities of Business* (Washington, D.C.: American Council on Education, 1961).

Settle, Theodore J. "Interaction between the Corporation and the University" (paper presented at the 1981 National Conference on Higher Education).

Smith, Norman R. "Corporate Training and The Liberal Arts" *Phi Delta Kappan*, January 1980.

Stone, Mildred F. *A Calling and Its College: A History of the American College of Life Underwriters* (Homewood, Ill.: Richard D. Irwin, 1963).

Stone, Mildred F. *The Teacher Who Changed an Industry: A Biography of Dr. Solomon S. Huebner* (Homewood, Ill.: Richard D. Irwin, Inc., 1960).

Tatel, David and Claire Guthrie. "The Legal Ins and Outs of University-Industry Collaboration" *Educational Record*, Spring 1983, 19-25.

154

Training Programs and Tuition Aid Plans. Personnel Policies Forum Survey No. 123 (Washington, D.C.: Bureau of National Affairs, 1978).

Tsurumi, Yoshi. "Too Many U.S. Managers are Technologically Illiterate" *High Technology*, April 1984, 14, 16.

"U.S. Training Census and Trends Report, 1982" *Training, HRD*, October 1982, 16-90.

Watkins, Beverly T. "Higher Education Now Big Business for Big Business." *The Chronicle of Higher Education*, April 13, 1983, 1, 6.

Weinstein, Laurence M. "Collecting Training Cost Data" *Training and Development Journal*, August 1982, 31-34.

"What To Do About American Schools" *Fortune* (special report) September 19, 1983.

Whitlock, Suzanne. *Education Programs in Industry: Case Studies—IBM Entry Level Marketing Training and Rust International, Inc.* (unpub. diss., The University of Alabama, 1982).

Woodington, Donald. "Some Impressions of the Evaluation of Training in Industry" *Phi Delta Kappan*, January 1980, 326-328.

155

INDEX

accreditation. *See* Curriculum, quality of; degrees, academic

adult learning resources, 2, 20-22, 133, 140

American Association of Community and Junior Colleges, 16

American Bankers Association, 113

American College (Pennsylvania), 87, 88, 97, 98, 99, 101, 102-105, 121

American College of Life Underwriters. *See* American College

American Council on Education, 80, 81

American Graduate School of International Management, 87-88, 98, 99, 120

American Institute of Banking (Boston), 88, 97, 100, 101-102, 113-115, 120

American Institute of Banking (New York), 62

American Management Associations, 40, 57, 88, 101, 116, 118

American Society for Training and Development, 6, 8, 52

Anderson, Robert O., 67-68. *See also* ARCO

Apollo, 108

Apple University Consortium/Corporation, 106, 130

ARCO (Atlantic Richfield Corporation), 48, 67-68

Arthur D. Little, 88, 97, 98, 100, 116, 121

Aspen Institute for Humanistic Studies, 66-67

Association for Media-Based Continuing Education for Engineers, 17, 86-87, 101

AT&T (American Telephone & Telegraph), 8, 14, 42, 67, 80

Baker, Jeanette S., 82-83

Baldwin, Lionel. *See* NTU

Barnard, Chester I., 41, 43

Baughman, James P., 69-70

Beard, Charles A., 35

Bell and Howell: DeVry Institutes of, 88, 97-98, 99, 116-117, 118

Bell System program, 8, 41, 43, 44, 66

Bell Telephone Laboratories, 108

Bendix Corporation, 96

Berkeley, University of California at, 113

Bigelow, Charles H., 34

Birbeck, George B., 30

Bloch, Erich, 3

boarding house system, 27-28

Boeing Aircraft Corporation, 17

Bok, Derek, 70

Boston Architectural Center, 88

Bowling Green State University, 79

Branscomb, Lewis, 123

Buffalo, State University of New York at, 126

business schools, 16-17, 69-70. *See also* name of school or university affiliation; universities

Business-Higher Education Forum: proposals of, 137-38

California State University system, 40, 112-113, 130

Calspan Corporation, 126

Carleton College, 44

157

Carnegie Institute of Technology, 38, 131
Carnegie, Andrew, 31
Carnegie-Mellon University, 31, 113, 131
Center for Public Resources: "Basic Skills in the U.S. Work Force," 6-7, 60-61, 125
Chartered Life Underwriter (CLU). *See* American College
Cheney Brothers Silk Mills, 34-35
Chicago, University of, 40
Chrysler Corporation, 62
Cincinnati, University of, 38
Clark, Harold F.: *Classrooms in the Factories* (with Harold S. Sloan), 42
CLU (Chartered Life Underwriter). *See* American College
College of Insurance (New York), 88, 99
Colorado, University of, 130
Columbia University, 70
Commission on Industrial Competitiveness, 138
community colleges, 16, 21, 100, 115, 136
Comprehensive Education and Training Act, 136
Consolidated Edison Company, 62, 82
Control Data Corporation, 11, 61, 80, 86, 101, 103, 104, 129-130
corporate education: distribution of, 9-10, 98; educational structure of, 49-51, 101, 116, 118-119; enrollment in, 7-8, 42, 97-98; expenditures for, 5-7, 8-9, 42; facilities, 47-49, 99-101; history of, 25-45; learning research and, 55-58; reasons for, 3-4, 12-14, 20; role in the company of, 51-52; teaching methods used in, 52-55. *See also* curriculum; industrialization, American; name of particular corporation or corporate center or institute; research and development; universities
Craig, Robert, 8
creative thinking courses, 43
credits: transfer of. *See* curriculum, quality of

Cremin, Lawrence A., 32
Cross, Patricia, 15
curriculum, corporate education: compared to traditional college curriculum, 76-79; compensatory education and the, 12; evaluation of, 120-121; general education and the, 75-76; human relations and the, 40-41, 43-44; humanistic studies and the, 48, 66-68; in 1950s and 1960s, 42-43; management and executive training, 39-45, 63-71; quality of, 79-83; sales, service, and customer training, 73-74; technical training, 71-73. *See also* degrees, academic; name of corporation or corporate center or institute

Dana Corporation/University, 48, 52, 54, 79, 80
Dartmouth College, 38, 44
Data General, 106
DeCarlo, Charles: *Education in Business and Industry* (with Robinson), 10
Defense, U.S. Department of, 87
degrees, academic, 85-121. *See also* curriculum, quality of; name of corporation or corporate center or institute
Delaware, University of, 129
delivery systems. *See* corporate education, structure of; NTU; teaching methods
Della Vos, Victor, 32
DeVry Institutes (Bell and Howell), 88, 97-98, 99, 116-117, 118
Digital Equipment Corporation, 11, 57, 74, 86, 106, 108, 128, 130-131
Dow Chemical: PLAN program of, 75
Dresser Industries, 80
Dulles, Foster Rhea, 27

Eddy, Bob, 56-57
education: implications of corporate education for, 64-65, 76-78, 124-127; industrialization and public, 30-33, 35-36; research and development and, 3, 10-

158

11, 22; work and public, 30-33. *See also* Mann, Horace; public policy; universities

Encyclopedia Britannica Educational Corporation, 118

engineering programs. *See* technical training

enrollment, corporate education, 7-8, 42, 97-98. *See also* name of corporation or corporate institute

evaluation. *See* degrees, academic

expenditures, corporate education, 5-7, 8-9, 42. *See also* name of corporation or corporate institute

facilities, corporate education, 47-49, 99-101. *See also* name of corporation or corporate institute

factory system, 26-29

faculty, 119. *See also* trainers, corporate education

family scheme, 27

Federal Commission on National Aid to Vocational Education, 36

federal regulations: corporate education and, 14. *See also* public policy

Ford Foundation, 112

Ford Motor Company, 96

Forrester, Jay W., 47

Franklin Institute, 30

Frey, Donald N., 117. *See also* Bell and Howell

Galbraith, John Kenneth, 43

Galloway, Lee, 38

Gardiner, John, 23, 25

GE. *See* General Electric

general education, 75-76

General Electric, 37, 42, 69-70, 72-73, 77-78, 79, 80

General Motors Corporation, 16, 86. *See also* General Motors Institute

General Motors Institute: accreditation of,

97; admissions policies of, 97-98; enrollment at, 43, 98; facilities of, 99; degree status of, 98-99; development of, 41-42, 96; quality of instruction at, 82-83; teaching methods of, 100-101

Gilbert, Thomas F., 6

Gilmore, Paul, 123

Global Stakes: The Future of High Technology in America (Botkin et al.), 3, 138

Goldstein, Harold, 7

Gray, Paul E., 131. *See also* MIT

Greeley, Horace, 31, 139

Grumman Corporation, 117-118

Gulf and Western, 96

Hamburger University, McDonald's, 97, 98, 115, 116, 118, 119

Harvard University/Business School, 40, 41, 70, 106, 108, 113

Hechinger, Fred, 118

Henderschott, F.C., 37

Heritage Foundation: *Blueprint for Jobs and Industrial Growth*, 3-4, 137

Hewlett-Packard, 11, 54, 55, 72, 75, 86, 106, 126, 135

high technology. *See* research and development; technical training

higher education. *See* education; universities

Higher Education Act (1972), 23

Higher Education Directory, 87

Hodgkinson, Harold, 6

Holbrook, Jerusha, 28

Holiday Inn University, 48

Honeywell Corporation, 72, 106

Hoover Institution: *To Promote Prosperity*, 4

Huebner, Solomon S., 87. *See also* American College

human relations courses, 40-41, 43-44

humanistic studies, 66-68. *See also* general education

159

160

National Association of Life Underwriters, 105
National Association of Corporation Schools (NACS), 36-39, 40
National Association of Employment Managers, 39-40
National Cash Register. *See* NCR
National Education Corporation, 117
National Personnel Association. *See* American Management Associations
National Registry of Credit Recommendations (American Council of Education), 81
National Science Foundation, 10, 109
National Society for the Promotion of Industrial Education, 35
National Technological University. *See* NTU
NCR (National Cash Register), 37, 48, 54, 62, 79, 80, 86
New England Telephone Company, 48
New York Edison Company, 37
New York State Regents, 80, 81-82
New York University, 38
Norris, William, 129, 130. *See also* Control Data Corporation
Northrop Corporation/University, 41, 56-57, 96-97, 98, 99-100
Northrop, John. *See* Northrop Corporation/University
Northwestern University, 44
NTU (National Technological University), 17, 51, 88, 101

100 Best Companies to Work for in America, The (Levering, Moskowitz, and Katz), 4

Paepcke, Walter, 66-67
Pennsylvania, University of, 38, 40, 41, 43-44, 70, 105
Pew Memorial Trust, 112
Pittsburgh, University of, 38
PLAN program (Dow Chemical), 75

PLATO computerized system. *See* Control Data Corporation
Polaroid: courses offered by, 53-54, 62, 64, 75-76
Pomfret Manufacturing Company, 27
PONSI (Program on Noncollegiate Sponsored Instruction), 80-81
pre-retirement programs, 75-76
Prentice-Hall, 128-129
Prime Computer, 106
Princeton University, 108, 126
productivity: American industrialization and, 33-36
proprietary schools, 116-118
public policy: corporate education and, 2, 22-23; industrialization and, 33, 35-36; programs and, 136-141

Rand Corporation, 88, 97, 98, 100, 101, 108-113, 116, 120, 121
Raytheon Corporation, 106
RCA, 86
Reif, F., 56
Rensselaer Polytechnic Institute, 126-127
research and development, 3, 10-11, 22. *See also* technical training; universities, collaboration between industry and
research on learning, 55-58
retirement programs, 75-76
retraining: need for, 133-137
Robinson, Ormsbee: *Education in Business and Industry* (with DeCarlo), 10
Rockwell International, 96
Rochester, University of, 131
Rockefeller Foundation, 113
Runkle, John D., 32

sales, service, and customer training, 13, 73-74
Scott Instruments Corporation, 128
Scott, Walter Dill, 35
Seattle University, 17
Serbein, Oscar, 42
Sloan Foundation, 112

161

162